Reaching Teens Through Film and Music, Volume 2000

Jesus in Modern Media

Michael Scully, OFM Cap.

Films

• Amistad • As Good as It Gets • City of Angels • Hope Floats • Meet Joe Black • Patch Adams • Pleasantville • The Man in the Iron Mask • The Rainmaker • Titanic • Tomorrow Never Dies

Songs

• Angel • Back 2 Good • Believe • Busy Man • Every Morning • Fly Away • Hands • I Will Remember You • Kiss Me • Livin' La Vida Loca • Lullaby • Ordinary Life • Save Tonight • Slide • Somebody's Out There Watching • Thank U

Hi-Time*Pflaum
Dayton, OH 45449

Reaching Teens Through Film and Music, Volume 2000

Michael Scully, OFM Cap.
Administrative assistants: Lynn Bruce
Jean Finch
Jean Ross
Mary Winter

To one young person in particular
who is trying to live the way he should.
Jamie, don't give up!

And to the young people
who continue to teach me,
especially those at Thomas More Prep-Marian High.

ISBN 0-937997-60-9

CONTENTS

Films

Songs

(c denotes that the song will be found on the country charts.)

Preface

I'm happy that you have chosen this latest volume of the *Jesus in Modern Media* series. I maintain that media can be used in religious education, and this is my attempt to make it possible for you. However, I believe that we must "direct" the message of the media. The media usually are not directed toward anything good or bad. Unfortunately, artists, directors, actors, and authors are often more interested in monetary rewards than in altruistic ones. Therefore, the media in general do not have the same goals that we have. We should make it clear to our students that our intentions are not to entertain, although it is a good side effect. Our intentions are to bring God closer to them by means of the popular media. I think the best way to do this is with the use of Scripture.

I cannot stress enough the importance of the use of Scripture for religious education, whether in Catholic school or parish religious education programs. I believe that the essential message is that we need to learn to live better. Scripture teaches us to do that.

Therefore, Scripture plays an extremely important part in this volume and all the volumes of the *Jesus in Modern Media* series. I urge you to give proper respect and attention to the word of God. Perhaps a special place of honor can be given to the Bible so that the young people will understand its importance.

Although the songs and movies deal with subjects that may not be found in sacred Scripture, Scripture has thoughts for every topic. The religious educator who uses this volume can even add to the Scripture passages listed for each song or movie session, or give a homily concerning a Scripture passage. Young people should understand that sacred Scripture is our textbook, and all other techniques we use in class are only part of a better understanding of the textbook.

With this edition, I am presenting both songs and movies in the same volume. This volume contains songs that were in the top five since October of 1998. It also contains movies that have been released in video since the summer of 1998.

I always find myself choosing my personal favorites in whatever volume of the *Jesus in Modern Media* series, thinking that you might be interested in how I would use those personal favorites.

The easiest songs to present are from the country chart because the songs are so direct in their approach. There are two rock songs that I would have a good time building a class around: "Hands" by Jewel, and "Thank U" by Alanis Morissette. Using the song "Hands," a class can easily be created to show that God uses us in his work. Using the thoughts of the song "Thank U," we can show young people how important it is to take time by themselves.

Among the movies, it is very difficult for me to choose a favorite because I believe every one of them can be used effectively. If I had to choose two favorites, they would be *Patch Adams* and *Pleasantville*. I think the movie *Titanic* would also make a good presentation simply because of its popularity.

I hope you enjoy working with the songs and movies. I have challenged you before, and I continue to challenge you to choose your own songs and movies to present. The "method" here is one that can be used in your own work.

Good luck! I believe that God will bless your life because you are a religious educator. The salvation of our young people depends on people like you!

Mike Scully
August, 1999

The Use of Popular Films in Youth Ministry

One of the most interesting documents resulting from the Second Vatican Council was entitled *Gaudium et Spes*, the *Pastoral Constitution on the Church in the Modern World*. The Council Fathers chose to address the subject of the "world and modern people." Never before had an official Church document looked at the subject in quite the same way. The document reflected on modern life and offered pastoral statements.

One statement from this document can be applied to modern media. The Council Fathers wrote in their introductory statement:

> ...the Church has always had the duty of scrutinizing the signs of the times and of interpreting them in the light of the gospel. Thus, in language intelligible to each generation, she can respond to the perennial questions that [people] ask about this present life and the life to come, and about the relationship of the one to the other. We must therefore recognize and understand the world in which we live, its expectations, its longings, and its often dramatic characteristics."
>
> *Gaudium et Spes*, the *Pastoral Constitution on the Church in the Modern World*, article 4

To recognize and understand the world in which young people live, we must look at films—one of the major forms of entertainment for American youth. Therefore, the duty of the religious educator, as the representative of the Church, is to "scrutinize" films and interpret them in the "light of the gospel."

There are numerous ways of going about the task. Many choose to take a negative attitude, declaring that the modern film has nothing significant to offer in light of the gospel. I think such an approach is not profitable, and the premise on which it is based is not true. Every modern film has a message, even if it seems totally inane. And because the Scriptures tell us about every aspect of life in one way or another, it is possible to relate a Scripture passage to the message of almost any film. That is the approach this resource book takes.

This book, as does each of the other books in the *Jesus in Modern Media* series, emphasizes that modern media provide a means to teach our junior high, senior high, and college youth. It suggests a method that uses the film without alteration, scrutinizing it in light of the gospel.

I feel that such an approach is not only useful, but absolutely necessary to reach the young person of today. A critic in one of the nation's leading media magazines, *Variety*, writes: "While TV networks, radio programs, the music world, magazines, and the video world cater to the young, the strongest attempt to win the minds and souls of young people probably occurs in the film industry." Should not religious educators, then, in scrutinizing the signs of the times, capitalize on the influence of this medium of entertainment with the intention of exploring what it has to offer in light of the gospel?

Hundreds of films are produced every year. Although all of them can, and perhaps should, be scrutinized in light of the gospel, there are many that fall into the category I refer to as "teaching films," which have a message for everyone. The films that I have chosen for this book make significant statements to young people in particular.

We remain in difficult times in the field of religious education. Most of us do not operate in a Catholic school setting on a junior high, senior high, or college level. We do not have the opportunity every day or every other day to teach the young people we so desperately want to educate. We see them at most once a week. How do we give quality education on religion—a subject that is most important of all—given the time constraints?

This book is my contribution to a solution. The idea is simple. Take the popular films that almost every teenager has already seen and relate them to Scripture, showing how Scripture has something to say in the same area that the film is considering. The films treated in this volume are recent releases and some of them have been honored with an award from the motion picture industry. Consequently, they qualify as "good" films in one way or another.

The general themes of these films can be easily arranged to provide either the sole content of a yearlong course of religious education or supplemental material for a course. Because most major concerns of a young person are illustrated by the films contained in this and every other volume of *The Message of Film*, the religious educator can use these films to help young people to a Christian understanding of their concerns. Consequently, I believe that this is a good way to educate our youth. I would go so far as to say that it is an essential way.

1. The average American teenager sees at least one movie a week either in a theater or on home video. Therefore, movies exercise an incredible amount of power in speaking to teenagers.
2. Using films in the religious education of teenagers is a way of gaining their attention. Young people already like movies. Religious educators today understand that they are competing with real professionals when it comes to gaining attention. Young people are constantly exposed to high quality presentations in theaters, on television and radio. Why not use the talents of those who make excellent films?
3. Young people will probably know the film chosen, and, therefore, knowledge of the life situation—a significant part of a lesson to be taught—is automatic.
4. Almost every good film—and certainly every film included in this volume—has some type of a God-figure or Jesus-figure. The awareness that a modern secular film contains such an image can have a powerful impact on young people.
5. Every educator at one time or another has experienced difficulty in conveying a particular concept. It is often much easier to refer to a film that expresses the idea. The film portrays the concept and provides the opportunity for discussion of the idea.
6. It is a well-known axiom that a picture is worth a thousand words. An idea portrayed on the screen generally has much greater impact than an instructor's vocal presentation.
7. Movies often have many themes running through them, and frequently one of the minor themes is important to a young person. Such a topic, suggested by viewing a film, may never have come up in a regular religion class.
8. Almost every film contains some type of violence or sexual activity. These topics must be addressed with today's teens, and a good film will usually provide the opportunity of discussing the topics directly.
9. Using films in the classroom or parish religious education setting promotes a positive attitude toward the media. The discussion of a film may help young people develop a more critical and selective approach to media in general.
10. Using movies tends to promote participation in three important ways. First, using films can attract young people to high school religion courses, religious education classes, and youth ministry sessions. Second, working with films also encourages young people's active participation during these classes or sessions. Teens who find it difficult to talk about their own problems find it easier to talk about other people's problems. Third, their discussions with young people can help religious educators understand and meet the needs of young people.

A Method of Using the Films Presented in This Book

I start with the premise that popular films should be used in youth ministry. In my own high school religious education courses, I use much of what the media offers—music, rock videos, television, commercials, and films. I work with all of these "in light of the gospel," that is, with Scripture. So I come to you with this approach field-tested. The young people to whom I have ministered seem to like this approach to religious education.

This material also could be used for the personal growth of religious educators, even though it is not written with that in mind. Making use of this material as personal meditation will enable a person not only to enjoy the movie, but also to grow spiritually. But the main purpose of this material is for teaching junior high, senior high, and college youth.

If you meet with teens every day or every other day, plan to spend a whole week or perhaps two on the material for one film. You will have the luxury of allowing a significant amount of time for personal reflection, written reports, and quality discussion. When I taught religion every day, I found that covering the material for four films was just about right for a semester.

Most religious educators who will use this resource book, however, will only have one or two hours a week. It is with this in mind that the material was written. I believe you can profitably devote a whole year of study to films. Choose four or five films for each semester according to the themes you want to present. The **General Theme** for each film gives an idea of the content of the film, and you can easily select films to cover whatever areas you want.

Another method, and perhaps the best way of using films in religious education, is to use only one or two to supplement the material that you are presenting. In that case again, the **General Theme** will help you choose which films would best fit your plan. See the index of Christian themes, pages 82-85.

I summarize sections of the *Catechism of the Catholic Church* to begin the presentation of each session. Use of the *Catechism* enables the instructor to state exactly what the Church teaches about a theme before teens see how the movie presents the theme.

A word of caution about the use of films with younger adolescents. The less mature the young person, the more the religious educator must do to teach with the film. Younger teens will want to concentrate on enjoying the movie and may miss what the educator is trying to do.

I have found it very helpful to invite other adults to take part in the presentation. They can be extremely helpful in the discussions by providing different points of view.

Following are guidelines for the format of a session. Feel free to adapt these quidelines to your own style and the needs of the group you are working with.

1. Rent or purchase the videocassette of the film. Preview the whole film before you begin the first session because it is good for you to know what is coming. But do not give away the plot in case teens have not seen the film or have forgotten it. The **Preliminary Thought** questions are written with that caution in mind. Concentrate on one session at a time. Trying to deal with too much material at once will prevent deeper discussion. You may even want to extend the session over a longer time than suggested.
2. Begin the session with some quiet time to emphasize that God is very much a part of the presentation. Then have a volunteer, either a teen or an adult, read the **Scripture**. Provide some quiet time for reflection after the reading so that the Scripture can make an impact.

3. Read the **Doctrine/Application**. You may want to make changes according to what you feel your particular group needs.
4. Use one or more of the **Preliminary Thought** questions. Read each question and give young people a few minutes to formulate their own answers. Young people may find it helpful to write their answers. You may also want to write some of your own questions, saving them in the space allowed for **Notes**. After teens have had a chance to come up with their own answers to these questions, ask them to share their answers. This fifteen- to twenty-minute discussion will lead into the presentation of the film. But before you begin to show the film, tell young people what you want them to look for as they view the film. Summarize the story line of the portion of the film that they will be seeing. Answer any questions teens may have.
5. To allow teens to focus on what they are seeing, show the appropriate portion of the film without comment.
6. If there are more than twelve participants, ask teens to form groups of five or six. Ask members of each group to take two or three minutes to write their answers to the first question in **Reflection/Ideas/Discussion**. After everyone has had a chance to write an answer, allow members of the group to discuss their answers.
7. Ask the groups to consider the rest of **Reflection/Ideas/Discussion**.

This book is meant to put me out of business. You can easily see how I have worked with these films. There may be other films that you want to present using the same method. I encourage you to do so.

Amistad

(This film is rated R by the motion picture industry because of violence and brief scenes of nudity. It is recommended for older adolescents only.)

General Theme

Historically, the practice of slavery is one of the worst evils that human beings have inflicted on one another.

SESSION I

From: Begins right away.
To: After Gibbs says, "Oh, he said, 'We have to go away.'"
Approximate time: 39 minutes

Theme: All people have a right to be free.
Scripture: Galatians 4:4-9—Christians are no longer slaves, but children of God.

Doctrine/Application

(Refer to the *Catechism of the Catholic Church,* paragraphs 1731-1738.)
It was clear to Saint Paul that if the early Christian community focused too narrowly on the law, they would lose perspective of what it meant to be free and thus become slaves again. In Paul's mind, slavery was one of the worst evils. He warns:

> *So you are no longer a slave but a child, and if a child then also an heir, through God. Formerly, when you did not know God, you were enslaved to beings that by nature are not gods...How can you want to be enslaved to them again?"*
>
> Galatians 4:7-9

The movie *Amistad* is the story of human beings forced into slavery by other human beings. It shows that each person has the right to freedom, and that no one has the right to take away another's freedom. During this first segment of the film, Cinque and his companions violently overcome the slavery into which they have been forced. The slaves knew that they were meant to be free; they knew that their captors were wrong, and so they took regaining their freedom into their own hands.

All human beings have the right to be free. Justice calls for this right to be recognized, but throughout history, human beings have violated this right. Some have forced others to be their slaves; some have freely chosen to be slaves to things. In North American society today, there is very little slavery in which one gives away one's freedom to another. But there is much slavery to things. Many have allowed pleasure and power to rule their lives; others have turned to money and have become slaves to it. Since Christians are called to break the shackles of the chains that take away their freedom, they are called to confront the modern slavery that is binding their spirits. They are called to accept the spirit of Jesus into their hearts, live as children of God, and thus gain the real freedom that leads to living fully.

Preliminary Thought

1. Why is slavery wrong?
2. Do slaves have the right to regain their freedom if that means killing their oppressors? Why or why not?
3. Explain the meaning of the phrase "becoming a slave to money."
4. How does accepting the spirit of Jesus lead to real freedom?

Notes

Reflection/Ideas/Discussion

What scene from this segment of the film is most striking? Why?

5. Scene analysis: The opening scene shows violence that will continue sporadically throughout the movie. Do you believe that the violence is depicted too graphically? Why or why not?
6. Scene analysis: Did the people who were held as slaves have the right to kill any of their captors? Why or why not?
7. Dialogue analysis. Martin Van Buren asked why he should be concerned about a few blacks. Obviously, Christians should always be concerned about those who are being oppressed. Do you think that politicians in general try to be concerned about everyone? Give examples to support your answer.
8. Dialogue/scene analysis: Adams refuses to help, saying, "Aim lower." This statement is probably telling the people who want something to happen to take care of it on "the local level." What one good thing could or do the people in your community accomplish without asking authorities for help?
9. Dialogue analysis: The remark is made that the slaves are people, not livestock. Do you know of any current situation in which people are not treated as dignified human beings? Give specific examples.
10. Scene analysis: The lawyers try to communicate with the Africans. Their attempt is made humorous by the subtitles that indicate misunderstanding on both sides. Is there anything that the lawyers could have done differently? What is the most important characteristic of communication?

Notes

SESSION II

From: After Gibbs says, "Oh, he said, 'We have to go away.'"
To: After Baldwin says to Cinque, "I need you to tell me how you got here."
Approximate time: 36 minutes

Theme: Using others is always wrong.
Scripture: John 8:2-11—The scribes and Pharisees use a woman to try to trick Jesus.

Doctrine/Application

(Refer to the *Catechism of the Catholic Church,* paragraphs 1829, 2196.)
One of the most touching stories in the gospels is about a woman who was caught in adultery. The scribes and the Pharisees brought the woman to Jesus, told him of her sin, and asked Jesus what he would say about it. Saint John tells us, "They said this to test him, so that they might have some charge to bring against him" (John 8:6). Jesus recognized what they were doing and would not allow himself to be deceived. The important part of the story, however, is the respect that Jesus shows for the woman. The scribes and Pharisees were merely using the woman to trick Jesus. Jesus does not approve of what the woman did and he does not agree with the attitude of the religious leaders, but he shows great respect for the person who sinned.

In *Amistad*, the Africans who were jailed in New Haven, Connecticut, after their attempt to regain their freedom were useful to others. A couple of groups wanted to lay claim to them because they could use them in some way. In particular, the American president, Martin Van Buren, wanted them given back to Spain so that he could be re-elected to the presidency. He tried everything he could legally do to return the Africans to slavery, using them to further his goal. For him, the Africans were objects to help satisfy selfish desires.

Selfish human beings will do anything to satisfy their desires. Perhaps the most dangerous attribute of selfishness is that many selfish people do not realize that they are selfish. They hurt people and use people and, in general, do not even realize that they are treating others badly. Using others for one's own interests is always wrong, but it may be one of the most common of all evils.

Preliminary Thought

11. Define "respect for another person." Give examples to support your answer.
12. Do you think that there are places in our world in which people are merely considered "objects" to be used? Give specific examples to support your answer.
13. Define "selfishness."
14. Do you agree with the statement that people who are selfish often do not even recognize it? Why or why not?

Notes

Reflection/Ideas/Discussion

What scene during this segment of the film is most striking? Why?

15. Scene analysis: Baldwin and Cinque seem to connect with one another even though they do not understand each other's words. Do you think that there are better ways of communicating than with words? Why or why not?
16. Scene analysis: The chains on board the *Amistad* appall Joadson. What are some things that have shocked you? Why?
17. Scene analysis: A man hits Baldwin. When we are doing something that others do not like, we must expect some type of persecution or retaliation. In your experience, what usually happens when someone is doing something right and another does not like it?
18. Analysis: Reference is made in this segment of the film to a person's "story." If "story" in this sense is understood as a philosophy of life, what elements would your philosophy or story of life include?
19. Dialogue/scene analysis: Baldwin, Joadson, and Cinque speak (through a translator) of Cinque's episode with the lion. The episode is important because it established Cinque as the leader. Cinque points out that he was not a "big man, but a lucky one." It has been said that most leaders become leaders because of some quirk of fate. Do you agree? Why or why not?
20. Scene analysis: Cinque remembers his wife. Memories are very important to human beings. What is the best memory you have of your past? Why is this memory so important to you?

Notes

SESSION III

From: After Baldwin says to Cinque, "I need you to tell me how you got here."
To: After Cinque yells at Baldwin, and the scene closes with Cinque's silhouette against the background of the fire.
Approximate time: 38 minutes

Theme: True Christianity is a source of hope for humankind, even in the most terrible circumstances.
Scripture: Revelation 5:6-10—Jesus' redemption of humankind is told in allegory form.

Doctrine/Application

(Refer to the *Catechism of the Catholic Church,* paragraphs 601-608.)
In a masterful scene during this segment of the movie, director Steven Spielberg shows how hope can come to the slaves who are now in jail in New Haven. One of the slaves explains Jesus

Christ's redemption of humankind to Cinque. Beginning with Jesus' healing powers and ending with his death on the cross, Cinque's fellow prisoner tells of Jesus' life and death. He also tells of Jesus' resurrection, ending with the hopeful words, "It doesn't look so bad."

At the same time that the grace of God is directing the slaves toward hope, God is leading the judge toward truth. The judge who was chosen to do what the President wanted—to send the slaves back to Spain—visits a church and, in the sacred surroundings that remind him of Jesus' death and resurrection, makes a decision that probably costs him his employment and maybe even his life. Spielberg seems to be saying that Jesus' redemption sets us free and leads us to truth.

Revelation 5:6-10 presents Jesus' redemption of humankind in allegory form. Jesus is represented by the Lamb who is praised: "You are worthy to take the scroll...for you were slaughtered and by your blood you ransomed for God saints from every tribe and language and people and nation" (Revelation 5:9). As a result, the seals of the scroll could be broken, and the scroll could be read. The scroll is a symbol of eternal life.

Christianity is a religion of great hope. Believing that Jesus Christ has redeemed us and has established a place in heaven for believers, Christians count on eternal life. Their belief should lead them to see the necessity of accepting the teachings of Jesus and directing their lives according to his will. The message of *Amistad* is that the grace of Jesus Christ leads to freedom and truth, that belief in Jesus can lead to salvation and a true understanding of life, no matter what kind of earthly life one has.

Preliminary Thought

21. What is your understanding of Jesus' redemption of humankind? Refer to paragraphs 604-606 of the *Catechism of the Catholic Church* for help.
22. It has been said that most Christians really do not understand what Jesus has done for us. Do you agree? Why or why not?
23. In your opinion, what is the principal teaching of Jesus Christ? Do you see this teaching lived out in your high school or college? Why or why not?
24. The meditation refers to the fact that believing in Jesus can lead to a true understanding of life. What do you think it means to have a true understanding of life?

Notes

Reflection/Ideas/Discussion

What scene during this segment of the film is most striking? Why?

25. Scene analysis: As Cinque remembers how he was taken as a slave, director Spielberg tries to be as realistic as possible, showing that the people were naked and beaten when they were made slaves. Does this offend you ? Why or why not? Do you think that the scene should be shown as realistically as it is? Why or why not?
26. Scene analysis: The one woman holds her child and falls overboard, taking her life and the life of her child. What is the significance of the scene?
27. Scene analysis: The women are drowned. How did you feel during this scene? Why?
28. Scene analysis: The people bid for the slaves. How do you think the slaves felt to be sold as if they were pieces of property?
29. Dialogue analysis: The opposing lawyer suggests that because some Africans have their own slaves, they accept slavery. Why did some of the Africans have slaves themselves?
30. Dialogue analysis: Cinque's yells, "Give us free." What is most striking about this scene? Why?
31. Scene analysis: Spielberg connects Jesus' redemption of humankind and the moral decision of the judge. What is the most important consequence that believing in Jesus should have for human beings?
32. Scene analysis: The judge decides in favor of the slaves. This decision probably had negative consequences for the judge, even though we don't learn about them from the film. In your opinion, are the judges of our court system this honest and courageous? Why or why not?
33. Dialogue analysis: On hearing the news that they must be tried again, Cinque says, "What kind of place is this? How can you live like this?" How would you explain the instances in which evil is committed, even in the court system?

Notes

SESSION IV

From: After Cinque yells at Baldwin, and the scene closes with Cinque's silhouette against the background of the fire.
To: End.
Approximate time: 35 minutes

Theme: People with righteousness on their side will always win, no matter what the outcome.
Scripture: Romans 1:16-17—The one who is righteous will live by faith.

Doctrine/Application

(Refer to the *Catechism of the Catholic Church,* paragraphs 1814-1816.)
What makes martyrs so sure of themselves? What makes people continue to believe even in the face of overwhelming odds? The answer may lie in the word "righteousness." If people are convinced that they are right, then their righteousness forces them to continue.

John Quincy Adams is about to argue on behalf of Cinque, the accused slave, and his companions. Adams explains that he will try to win the case because righteousness is on their side. While winning may not involve what human beings understand as victory, righteousness always brings about victory in the sense that God understands victory.

That's why Saint Paul tells the Romans, "The one who is righteous will live by faith" (Romans 1:17). As a matter of fact, the person who is righteous may die but, by living out faith, achieve eternal life. The Christian always believes that the outcome of any occasion will be good if righteousness is upheld. Even if John Quincy Adams could not free the slaves, he had to do what he did because he believed that slavery was wrong. In the same way, if we know that something is wrong, our faith calls for us to do what we can to correct the situation. And if righteousness is on our side, using the words of John Quincy Adams in this segment of *Amistad*, then we will win, no matter what the outcome.

Preliminary Thought

34. Who are some modern-day martyrs that you are aware of?
35. Define "righteousness." Give examples to support your definition.
36. Name an evil situation that you are aware of. What can you do about the situation?
37. In your opinion, what elements in the lifestyle of young people today is most in need of improvement? Is there anything you can do to bring about change?

Notes

Reflection/Ideas/Discussion

What scene during this segment of the film is most striking? Why?

38. Scene analysis: Adams tells the guard to unshackle Cinque to show trust. In general, do people trust other people enough? Why or why not?
39. Dialogue analysis: Adams asks Cinque whether he knows why he must go to the Supreme Court, and Cinque answers, "It is the place where they finally kill us." Obviously, this is a statement of cynicism. From what you know about the Supreme Court, do you think the Supreme Court plays a significant part in the way of life in the United States? Why or why not?
40. Dialogue analysis: Cinque tells Adams that the past is the reason why they exist at all. What do you think this means?
41. Dialogue analysis: Adams speaks to the Supreme Court about truth, the nature of man, slavery, and freedom. What part of the speech impresses you most? Why?
42. Dialogue analysis: Adams ends his speech with the statement that "who we are is who we were." What do you think he means?
43. Scene analysis: The Slave Fortress is liberated. One is reminded of the prison camps of Nazi Germany and of many other countries. Why do you think such places exist?
44. Scene analysis: The movie ends with a statement that many of Cinque's family probably had been sold into slavery, even though he returned a free man. This is a statement of despair because the slavery ring had not yet been broken. What do you think Cinque's future would be?
45. Analysis: What can we learn from *Amistad*?

Notes

As Good as It Gets

General Theme
Friendship can be a cure for illness.

SESSION I

From: Begins right away.
To: After Melvin asks the waiter for Carol's last name, and the waiter says, "Connelly."
Approximate time: 44 minutes

Theme: If we try to understand people with problems, we may find them to be caring people.
Scripture: John 9:1-7, 35-38—Jesus chooses to give sight to a man.

Doctrine/Application
(Refer to the *Catechism of the Catholic Church*, pagragraphs 1431-1433.)
Most of the healing stories of the gospel begin with someone asking Jesus for help. Those asking may be people needing help or friends or relatives of people needing help. In some instances, however, Jesus deliberately chooses to help someone who has not asked for help. Such is the case with the man born blind (John 9: 1-7). The man happened to be near the path that Jesus and his disciples had chosen. Why did Jesus choose to cure him? Chances are that Jesus recognized the man as someone who would do something significant in the future. Perhaps he would be helpful to someone else. In fact, we see something of his character when he witnesses to what has happened to him (John 9:13-34). We also see his desire to believe in Jesus (John 9:35-38). The blind man was a person with problems who became a caring person as a result of the grace of God.

Melvin Udall was a person with problems. Anyone who knew him could easily verify that. He was a cranky, bigoted, verbally abusive man who cared only for himself. His personal problems were overwhelming, showing themselves in pronounced obsessive-compulsive behavior. As a result, it seemed that he would never be able to ease his arrogant attitude, even if he wanted to. Then some people and a dog came into his life. And suddenly, this bizarre human being actually began to care about others.

People with problems surround us. In fact, we all have problems. The people we know may not have problems like Melvin Udall's, but they have problems. Some feel rejected or deserted by their families. Some have chosen a life of rebellion. Some are lonely, and some are depressed because of lack of love. At the same time, we know that all of these people possess the capability to be concerned people. Part of Christian love is giving others the opportunity to care by showing them how much we care for them.

Preliminary Thought

1. In your opinion, what is the principal reason for Jesus' miracles?
2. As you look at the people in your neighborhood, what problems do you find? What can be done about these problems?
3. How can one young person help another young person who has a serious problem? Give specific examples.

Notes

Reflection/Ideas/Discussion

What scene during this segment of the film is most striking? Why?

4. Dialogue analysis: Simon says to Melvin,"You don't love anything, Mr. Udall." Do you believe that there are people who really do not love anybody or anything? Why?
5. Scene analysis: Melvin has problems. Although we do not see many people like this, what is the best way to deal with people who have severe problems?
6. Dialogue/scene analysis: Melvin becomes very angry with Simon and verbally insults and abuses him. If you would receive the type of tirade that Melvin gave Simon, how do you think you should respond?
7. Scene analysis: Simon is homosexual. How do you feel about homosexuality? To learn what the Church teaches about homosexuality, refer to articles 2357-2359 of the *Catechism of the Catholic Church*. What is your reaction to this teaching? Why?
8. Scene analysis: Obviously, Melvin is prejudiced against African Americans. Is prejudice a problem at your school right now? Why or why not?
9. Scene analysis: Melvin displays bizarre behavior in the restaurant. Most restaurant owners or managers would not tolerate this type of behavior. Why do you think no one did anything to try to correct Melvin's behavior?
10. Scene analysis: Carol and her boyfriend immediately go into lovemaking activity. Most dates do not begin with lovemaking and sex, but many do. Why does the Church consider this kind of casual sexual activity sinful?
11. Scene analysis: Simon's apartment is robbed. Why are there so many robberies in our country?
12. Scene analysis: Verdell, the dog, makes an impression on Melvin. Why do pets often seem to affect cranky people for the better?

13. Scene analysis: The dog avoids the cracks in the sidewalk just as Melvin does. The action is an exaggeration called for by the director, but it is often reported that animals take on certain characteristics of their owners. Do you believe that this can be true? Why or why not?
14. Scene analysis: Melvin goes to see his psychiatrist. The psychiatrist has a difficult time with him. In general, do you believe that psychiatrists can help people who are as disturbed as Melvin is? Why or why not?
15. Dialogue analysis: Melvin shouts at the people in the psychiatrist's office, "What if this is as good as it gets?" What do you think he meant by this?

Notes

SESSION II

From: After Melvin asks the waiter for Carol's last name, and the waiter says, "Connelly."
To: After Melvin says to Simon and Carol, "Tomorrow, you'll see if you can get another big wad of sweaty money out of his hand."
Approximate time: 46 minutes

Theme: We become better persons when we are interested in others.
Scripture: 1 John 3:15-18—To be Christians, we must love others.

Doctrine/Application

(Refer to the *Catechism of the Catholic Church*, paragraphs 1822-1829.)
In *As Good As It Gets,* Melvin Udall realized that he had some serious problems. He recognized that he needed the help of a psychiatrist, but, at the same time, he felt hatred and disgust for others. During this segment of the movie, something was beginning to change inside him. Maybe the change was caused by the feelings he had for the dog or for Carol, the waitress. He didn't know for sure what was happening, but he gradually began to see that he needed to be interested in others.

"We know love by this, that he laid down his life for us—and we ought to lay down our lives for one another" (1 John 3:16). We learn from this that showing love for others is the way to begin changing ourselves for the better. We all must change something in our lives, no matter who we are. In the first century, the great philosopher Seneca wrote: "The evil which assails us is not in the localities we inhabit, but in ourselves." We all struggle with evil. Perhaps we ought to attack the evil within us by reaching out to others, recognizing that we really can help them. Showing love for others can be the road to personal conversion.

Preliminary Thought

16. Do you think that most people who others see as "mean" know that they are mean? Why or why not?
17. In your school or community, are there problems that could be solved if people were to reach out to others?
18. "We all struggle with evil." Do you agree? Why or why not?

Notes

Reflection/Ideas/Discussion

What scene during this segment of the film is most striking? Why?

19. Dialogue analysis: Carol says to Melvin, "Don't you have any control on how creepy you get?" Do you think Melvin can control his behavior? Why or why not?
20. Scene analysis: Evidently, Carol could not get proper care for her son Spencer because they did not have enough money or adequate health insurance. Do you think this is a true picture of what happens in real life? Why or why not?
21. Scene analysis: The doctor reveals to Carol that Melvin is paying for Spencer's care. In your opinion, what was Melvin's motivation?
22. Dialogue/scene analysis: Carol tells Melvin that she will not sleep with him. Why do people automatically assume that a person who is doing something good for them will want something in return?
23. Scene analysis: Melvin takes some soup to Simon. In your opinion, what was Melvin's motivation?
24. Dialogue/scene analysis: Carol's mother does not understand Carol's depression. What can a young person do for someone who seems to be depressed?
25. Dialogue/scene analysis: Why do you think Melvin does not want to be thanked?
26. Scene analysis: Simon tells his story. Do you believe things that happen to people can make them homosexual? Why or why not?
27. Dialogue analysis: Melvin says that anger is caused not so much by the terrible things that happen as by the fact that others have it so good. Do you agree? Why or why not?

Notes

SESSION III

From: After Melvin says to Simon and Carol, “Tomorrow, you’ll see if you can get another big wad of sweaty money out of his hand.”
To: End.
Approximate time: 45 minutes

Theme: Sometimes deep problems can be cured by friendship.
Scripture: Mark 2:13-17—Jesus calls Levi (Matthew).

Doctrine/Application

(Refer to the *Catechism of the Catholic Church,* paragraphs 1939-1942.)
At first glance, Melvin Udall and Levi don’t seem to have much in common. Levi becomes known as Matthew and gives his life to the cause of Jesus Christ. It seems as if Melvin has no cause at all except himself. But upon closer consideration, there may be a resemblance.

Matthew was a tax collector. Other Hebrews hated him because he had accepted a job with the unpopular Romans. At the same time, he exacted more money than necessary and thus enjoyed a good living. Liked by neither the Romans nor the Hebrews, he was undoubtedly a disgruntled, maybe even angry, man. Matthew’s friendship with Jesus, however, changed everything.

Melvin Udall was a man with serious problems. He knew only hate from the people around him. Although he may not have realized it completely, he had been doing things all of his life that turned people against him. Suddenly, there were people he cared about. He could not explain it, but he wanted to help those people. The growing friendships began to change him.

We all have problems that we try to address in our lives. Sometimes, these problems overwhelm us, practically immobilizing us. Sometimes, our problems are simple to resolve. The examples of Matthew in the gospels and Melvin Udall in *As Good As It Gets* can help us understand that an important part of overcoming problems is establishing and maintaining friendships with others. Being a friend to someone takes our attention away from ourselves.

Preliminary Thought

28. The meditation discusses the importance of friendship. In your opinion, what two or three elements are necessary to being a friend to someone?
29. What are the most serious problems a young person must deal with in today’s world?
30. Some people maintain that there are only a few really good friends in everyone’s life. Do you agree? Why or why not?

Notes

Reflection/Ideas/Discussion

What scene during this segment of the film is most striking? Why?

31. Dialogue/scene analysis: Melvin insults Carol in the restaurant. Why do you think he said what he did?
32. Dialogue analysis: Melvin says to Carol, "You make me want to be a better man." In what way does friendship make people want to be better?
33. Dialogue/scene analysis: Melvin admits to Carol that he finds it exhausting to open up to other people. It is extremely difficult for a person with an obsessive-compulsive personality to admit mistakes. Admitting to mistakes is difficult for everyone. In your opinion, why is it so difficult for human beings to admit their mistakes?
34. Scene analysis: Simon paints portraits of Carol. These scenes involve some nudity. Do you think that there should be nudity in movies? Why or why not? Do you think nudity in films affects young people? Why or why not?
35. Dialogue analysis: Carol says that Simon gave her what she needed. What do you think Carol needed most of all?
36. Dialogue analysis: Simon counsels Melvin to tell Carol about his feelings for her. Why is it difficult to express one's feelings to another?
37. Dialogue/scene analysis: Melvin forgot to lock the door because he was preoccupied with his feelings toward Carol. Also, he forgets to put on gloves when he must touch something. These actions seem to indicate that Melvin's condition is improving. Do you think Melvin will ever be able to get back to normal behavior? Why or why not?
38. Dialogue analysis: Carol and Melvin both agree to the statement, "Maybe we could live without the wisecracks." Wisecracks can cause serious problems between people. If a friend of yours has the habit of using wisecracks, what can you do to help this person?
39. Scene analysis: In the last scene, Melvin finally steps on a crack. In your opinion, what will his future be like? Do you think Carol and Melvin could get married and live happily ever after? Why or why not?
40. Analysis: What lesson can we learn from the movie *As Good As It Gets*?

Notes

City of Angels

General Theme

People (and angels) must use their free will wisely and always with love as a guide.

SESSION I

From: Begins right away.
To: When Maggie and Seth are in the library, and Seth says, "I'm a messenger of God."
Approximate time: 37 minutes

Theme: Some things are true whether you believe in them or not.
Scripture: Matthew 18:10-14—There are lost sheep that must be found.

Doctrine/Application

(Refer to the *Catechism of the Catholic Church*, paragraphs 328-336.)
The *Catechism of the Catholic Church* tells us that "Angels have been present since creation and throughout the history of salvation, announcing this salvation from afar or near and serving the accomplishment of the divine plan" (paragraph 332). The foundation for this statement comes from Scripture. In fact, it can be argued that each of us has his or her own angel. Jesus tells us that even the "little ones" have angels who "continually see the face of my Father in heaven" (Matthew 18:10).

There is no better modern presentation of this doctrine than in the movie *City of Angels*. Accepting the existence of angels without any hesitation, the movie shows that angels, like human beings, have free will. The angel Seth says to the incredulous Maggie, "Some things are true whether you believe in them or not." Of all the problems with faith, the most fundamental is the lack of scientific proof. Many good scientists even debate the existence of God. Likewise, we have no record, other than the Scriptures, of anyone seeing or interacting with an angel. In fact, Christians would be hard-pressed to prove scientifically that Jesus Christ was the Son of God. In the same way, non-Christian religions would be hard-pressed to prove their central doctrines. The believer must simply believe. We should have reason to believe, of course, but, in the final analysis, a believer accepts Christian teaching based on faith, not scientific proof.

In *City of Angels*, Maggie gradually becomes a believer. We are also called to become believers and to live our lives according to our beliefs.

Preliminary Thought

1. How do you feel about the Christian belief concerning angels?
2. Consider the statement of Seth in the movie: "Some things are true whether you believe in them or not." What are some instances in which this statement is true? Give specific examples.
3. What is the most important fact of our religion that we believe without scientific proof?
4. The meditation says that we must live our lives according to our beliefs. What should be most apparent in the life of someone who believes in Jesus?

Notes

Reflection/Ideas/Discussion

What scene during this segment of the film is most striking? Why?

5. Scene analysis: The Christian doctrine of eternal life brings us hope. We obviously know nothing about what happens after death, but it is presented in such a mild way in the movie that it is not a "scary" thing. What do you think happens after death?
6. Dialogue analysis: Seth tells the little girl that her mother will understand the girl's death someday. How do you think a believer would look at the death of a young person? How do you think a nonbeliever would look at that death?
7. Scene analysis: Angels are everywhere. The movie shows the existence of angels, and especially guardian angels, in a striking way. What did you think as you looked at all the angels?
8. Scene analysis: The patient dies. We depend upon technology more and more and, therefore, live longer. In general, it is good that people live longer, but what are the disadvantages of a long life?
9. Scene analysis: During a robbery, the angels help, with Cassiel commenting, "They don't need to see us." The scene shows the grace of God at work. Do you believe that God's grace works to prevent evil? Why or why not?
10. Dialogue analysis: Maggie comments about who doctors are fighting when they try to save a person's life. In fact, they are fighting against disease that infects human beings simply because they are human. What lesson should a Christian learn from an illness?
11. Scene analysis: Anne tells Maggie about the baby she found in a dumpster. Unfortunately, this actually happens in our world. Why do you think someone might abandon a baby in a dumpster?

12. Dialogue analysis: Seth tells Maggie that the patient she lost is alive. Seth is talking about eternal life. Maggie says that she doesn't believe in eternal life. Why do you think some people don't believe in eternal life?
13. Dialogue/scene analysis: Seth tells Maggie that he is a messenger of God. In your understanding, how are angels God's messengers to us?

Notes

SESSION II

From: When Maggie and Seth are in the library, and Seth says, "I'm a messenger of God."
To: When Messinger and Maggie are talking, and Messinger says, "Because I did it."
Approximate time: 36 minutes

Theme: The beauty of being human is comparable to being heavenly.
Scripture: Psalm 8—The majesty of God and the dignity of man.

Doctrine/Application

(Refer to the *Catechism of the Catholic Church*, paragraphs 1700-1709.)
Central to the *City of Angels* is a love relationship between Seth, an angel of God, and Maggie, a human being. To be sure, it is unlikely and mere fantasy. But what seems to be more unlikely is the possibility that a heavenly creature would give up his spiritual nature in order to become human. In fact, it seems incredible that anyone who has the special gifts of heaven would want to give them up. But it leads to good meditation to look at such a desire.

In *City of Angels*, Seth possesses all the beauties of heaven, but he does not understand any of the human senses. As an angel, he also does not have the human ability to love another or to receive love from another. Obviously we don't know whether these are true charactertics of angels, but this description of Seth should make us think about what we possess as human beings.

Psalm 8:5-6 tells us that God has made human beings "a little lower than God, and crowned them with glory and honor" and "given them dominion over the works of [God's] hands, putting all things under their feet." God has given much to human beings. Also, God's gift of life does not stop with this life. Redeemed by God's Son, every human being can choose everlasting life and be eternally happy.

It would be good for us to recognize the gifts we have been given. If we did, maybe we would feel more obliged to take better care of our bodies, treating them with respect, and staying away from anything harmful. Perhaps we would also learn to regard the beautiful gift of sexual love of another with more respect.

Preliminary Thought

14. What do you think is the greatest human gift that we possess? Why?
15. What do we do that is most harmful to our bodies?
16. The meditation refers to respecting the gift of sexual love. What do you think that respect should mean to young people who are just beginning to have relationships with those of the opposite sex? What do you think that respect should mean to married people?

Notes

Reflection/Ideas/Discussion

What scene during this segment of the film is most striking? Why?

17. Scene analysis: All of the angels are watching Seth and his interaction with Maggie. Why do you think this is true?
18. Dialogue analysis: Jordan says to Maggie that he hopes that she will not become "one of those surgeons who prays in the OR." Why do you think he said that?
19. Dialogue analysis: Messinger tells Seth that "people don't believe in us anymore." Why do you think people refuse to believe in "things of heaven"?
20. Analysis: As you learn about Maggie and her beliefs, why do you think she does not believe in heavenly things?
21. Scene analysis: Seth does much soul-searching to determine whether he wants to give up his angel-life in order to become human. What would you find most attractive about Seth's angel-life?
22. Scene analysis: Maggie has sudden knowledge of why the baby could not sleep. In your opinion, how did she gain this knowledge?

Notes

SESSION III

From: When Messinger and Maggie are talking, and Messinger says, "Because I did it."
To: End.
Approximate time: 33 minutes

Theme: When one makes a choice, one must accept the consequences.
Scripture: Deuteronomy 30:15-20—Moses commands the Israelites to choose life.

Doctrine/Application

(Refer to the *Catechism of the Catholic Church*, paragraphs 2464-2470.)
Many choices are made with little or no thought about what will happen as a result. When choices that involve life or death are made, the consequences must be considered carefully. In light of this, the angel Seth is about to choose to exercise his free will as an angel and become a human being. *City of Angels* presents the agonizing thought that goes into his decision.

A decision to live in a certain way involves consequences. Moses tells the Israelites, "I have set before you life and death, blessings and curses. Choose life so that you and your descendants may live, loving the LORD your God, obeying him, and holding fast to him; for that means life to you and length of days...." (Deuteronomy 30:19-20). According to Moses, the Israelites' decision to choose life guided by the Commandments would carry with it consequences, the need to hold fast to the Lord's directives. The consequences of their decision would involve doing difficult things.

Seth the angel had to accept the consequences of his decision. Cassiel, his brother angel, tells him, "That's life. You're living now." Humanity has its rewards and consequences, some of which are difficult to accept. In the real world, we also make life and death decisions. There are consequences that follow making the choice to marry or making a solemn vow of celibacy. There are consequences of accepting the responsibility to be a best friend or confidant. We often sees examples of people who make serious decisions involving life and then try to escape the consequences. The example of Seth after his decision to become human is one that many people should study well.

Preliminary Thought

23. What are the most serious choices that a young person makes?
24. Choose one of these serious choices, and name all of the possible consequences.
25. The meditation tells us, "We often see examples of people who make serious decisions involving life and then try to escape the consequences." Describe such an example.

Notes

Reflection/Ideas/Discussion

What scene during this segment of the film is most striking? Why?

26. Scene analysis: Seth jumps off of the building, a sign of his decision to become human. Do you think that he prepared enough for the decision? Why or why not?
27. Scene analysis: Seth celebrates in the street, simply because he is alive and human. In general, are people happy to be alive? Why or why not?
28. Scene analysis: Seth is beaten up. Undoubtedly, director Brad Silberling is saying in this scene that this is part of real life. Do you believe that violence is just a part of life? Why or why not?
29. Dialogue analysis: Seth says that what he likes best about living is love. What do you like best about living? Why?
30. Scene analysis: Maggie is almost in a trance at the store and on her way back. In your opinion, what is the meaning of the scene?
31. Scene analysis: Before the accident and at the time of the accident, Seth and Maggie are connecting, even though they are apart. In your opinion, what is the meaning of their actions?
32. Dialogue/scene analysis: Cassiel and Seth talk about two questions that are commonly asked when tragedy happens. One, "Why did God allow this?" blames God for what happened. As a Christian, how would you answer the question?

    The other question is, "Am I being punished?" Cassiel says, "You know better than that." How would you answer that question?

    Finally, Cassiel says, "That's life. You're living now, and you'll be dying." What disturbs you most about dying?
33. Dialogue analysis: Seth talks about his love for Maggie: "I would rather have had one breath of her hair, one kiss from her mouth, one touch of her hand, than eternity without it. One." What strikes you most about his statement?
34. Closing scene: Seth is in the water and Cassiel is smiling. What do you think the director wants to convey with the scene?
35. Analysis: In your opinion, what is the most important lesson of *City of Angels*?

Notes

Hope Floats

General Theme

People can find hope in every situation.

SESSION I

From: Begins right away.
To: After Justin says to the waitress at the cash register, "Keep the change," and looks back at Birdee.
Approximate time: 36 minutes

Theme: While it is very difficult to overcome a major trauma in one's life, a person must keep trying.
Scripture: Matthew 26:73-75; 27:3-5—Peter and Judas react to the knowledge that they have betrayed Jesus.

Doctrine/Application

(Refer to the *Catechism of the Catholic Church*, paragraphs 2091-2092.)
How should people react to a serious mistake that they have made, especially when there seems to be no hope of changing the consequences of the mistake? In particular, what can they do when they must function in the immediate aftermath of the mistake? Peter and Judas both had to struggle with answers to those questions. Both had deliberately abandoned the person they had accepted as Lord. Both felt compelled to action because of their mistakes.

It is important to see why Peter became a saint and Judas felt condemned. Peter kept trying, while Judas gave up. Overcome with grief, Peter had the presence of mind to confront himself. He saw who he was in the sight of God, and so, "he went out and wept bitterly" (Matthew 26:75). Likewise overcome with the horror of his action, Judas could not endure his sin, and so, "he departed and he went and hanged himself" (Matthew 27:5). Peter faced up to the ordeal that separated him from his Lord; Judas did not.

There is probably nothing more painful in life than the feeling of despair. When some trauma enters our lives, it seems natural for us to feel sorry for ourselves and to want to hide.

In the movie *Hope Floats*, Birdee Pruitt was embarrassed beyond belief. Her husband was having an affair and admitted it to her in front of millions of people. Overcome with grief, she wanted to hide. She also wanted to protect her child from the accusing stares of neighbors and fallen-away friends.

There seemed to be two choices she could make. One might be called the "Peter choice"—to bear the pain, admit the situation, move on with life, and survive. The other could be called the "Judas choice"—to give up. Moving away from her home that she loved, Birdee felt more inclined to Judas' choice than to Peter's.

Preliminary Thought

1. What are some of the serious mistakes that people make in life? What can be done to recover from each of these mistakes?
2. Why do we not handle trauma very well?
3. What do you think you would actually do if something very embarrassing happened to you and your friends found out about it? What do you think is the best thing a person can do in a situation like this?

Notes

Reflection/Ideas/Discussion

What scene during this segment of the film is most striking? Why?

4. Scene analysis: Birdee's husband is on a television talk show. How do you feel about television talk shows? Do you believe that they are good entertainment? Why or why not?
5. Scene analysis: Bill and Birdee's daughter Bernice is crying. The separation which Bill and Birdee go through will affect Bernice adversely throughout the movie. Why do parents pay so little attention to their children when they are having difficulties with each other?
6. Character analysis: Ramona Calvert, Birdee's mother. From what you have seen of her so far, what kind of a person is she?
7. Dialogue/scene analysis: Birdee and her mom talk about what happened. From what you have seen so far, who do you think was most at fault in Bill and Birdee's failing relationship? Why?
8. Scene analysis: Birdee and her mother argue about whether Birdee feels sorry for herself. Specifically, what can be done to help people when they feel sorry for themselves?
9. Dialogue/scene analysis: Birdee visits an employment agency. We learn that when she was in high school, Birdee was not nice to those who were not popular. Why is popularity so important to high school students?

Notes

SESSION II

From: After Justin says to the waitress at the cash register, "Keep the change," and looks back at Birdee.
To: After Bernice looks at Birdee in the bathroom, and Bernice closes the door.
Approximate time: 35 minutes

Theme: Knowing an understanding person is important to someone who wants to start over after experiencing a trauma.
Scripture: Luke 19:1-10—Jesus tells Zacchaeus that he has earned salvation.

Doctrine/Application

(Refer to the *Catechism of the Catholic Church*, paragraphs 1830-1832.)
After Birdee's daughter Bernice has some difficulties in school, she comes home thoroughly depressed. In a very touching and unexpected way, Birdee, Travis, and Ramona try to cheer Bernice up. The scene shows how Justin is trying to help Birdee. It is not easy for Birdee to start over after experiencing her trauma, especially in the town in which she had the reputation of hurting others. An understanding person will be helpful to her.

Zacchaeus' reputation in Luke's gospel was one of hurting others. He was a chief tax collector, and he was probably guilty of what we now call extortion. He probably taxed his fellow Hebrews more than the Roman tax demanded so that he would be able to pay the Romans and also enjoy a good livelihood. But we are also led to believe that he was searching for something because we are told that he "was trying to see who Jesus was" (Luke 19:3). Perhaps he was reaching out to someone who would understand and help him.

We all want the understanding of others. We especially desire it when things are not going well in our lives. Traumas, large and small, happen to all of us, especially when we are discovering adult life. Christians will be aware of their own desire for understanding in moments of confusion. This awareness should move them to reach out to others who are suffering disturbances in their lives. To begin again after some trauma is not an easy task, and the person who does it must have the help and understanding of others.

Preliminary Thought

10. In your experience, how do young people in high school or college hurt other young people?
11. From reading the story of Zacchaeus, what do you think was lacking in his life? Why?
12. What does it mean to be understanding?

Notes

Reflection/Ideas/Discussion

What scene during this segment of the film is most striking? Why?

13. Scene analysis: Birdee's dad is an Alzheimer's patient. What is the best way to care for people who are losing their memories? Is placement in a nursing home the best possibility? Why or why not?
14. Scene analysis: Birdee's dad dances with Birdee. What do you think is the significance of this scene?
15. Character analysis: Bobbi-Claire seems like a "fake" person. From what you have seen of her so far, what do you think of her?
16. Dialogue analysis: Justin reminds Birdee that they were in different groups in high school. Why are there different groups or cliques in high school? Should young people work to eliminate groups that exclude people? Why or why not?
17. Scene analysis: Bernice has a problem with Big Dolores. What do you think should have been the solution to the problem?
18. Scene analysis: Justin and Birdee are at the closed outdoor theater. Justin says that he wishes he was sixteen again. Why do you think older people want to be sixteen again? Why does Birdee resist Justin's advances?
19. Scene analysis: Bernice is in a fight. What do you think an adult coming on this scene should have done?
20. Scene analysis: Birdee and the others cheer up Bernice. What are the good things that you see about this scene?
21. Dialogue analysis: Justin and Birdee talk about the American dream. In your opinion, what is the American dream? Is it good, bad or both? Why?
22. Scene analysis: Birdee and Justin seem to have had sex. Aside from the fact that their having sex would be a violation of a commandment, do you think that it was good for them to have physical relations at this time? Why or why not? Is there ever a case in which premarital sex or extramarital sex would not be a violation of the commandment of God? Why or why not?

Notes

SESSION III

From: After Bernice looks at Birdee in the bathroom, and Bernice closes the door.
To: End.
Approximate time: 38 minutes

Theme: If people can see hope in their lives, they can survive.
Scripture: Acts 2:22-28—There is real hope for the followers of Jesus.

Doctrine/Application

(Refer to the *Catechism of the Catholic Church,* paragraphs 1817-1821.)
In the beginning of this segment of *Hope Floats*, there does not seem to be much hope floating. Birdee cannot really feel the love of Justin, even though there is a physical attraction between them. Birdee is accused of putting up barriers to love. Bernice is having a very difficult time adjusting, both at school and at home. Birdee's father cannot help because of his Alzheimer's disease, and the strange household in which Birdee and Bernice live does not seem to offer any answers.

In fact, a comparison can easily be made between the Pruitt family problems and the problems of the early Christians. For the early Christians, there seemed to be little hope, but Peter reminds his fellow Christians that the opposite is true. Quoting a psalm of David, Peter challenges the Israelites to believe in Jesus: "...therefore my heart has been glad, and my tongue rejoiced; moreover my flesh will live in hope. For you will not abandon my soul to Hades....You have made known to me the ways of life" (Acts 2:26-28).

The ways of life finally become clearer for Birdee during this segment of *Hope Floats*. Although Birdee and her daughter are still experiencing trauma and confusion, life begins ever so slowly to make more sense. As Birdee's mother explains to Bernice, "God invented families so 'hopeless' doesn't get the last word."

The secret to viewing the world with hope, however, is to choose to view it with hope. The person who lives in despair may never have allowed hope to function. The movie closes with an excellent statement: "Beginnings are scary. Endings are usually sad, but it's what's in the middle that counts the most. You need to remember that when you find yourself at the beginning. Just give hope a chance to float up. And it will." That's good advice for all of us—if we give hope a chance to float up, it will.

Preliminary Thought

23. What can be done for people who find themselves with no hope?
24. Peter quotes the psalmist David who speaks of the "ways of life." What are the ways of life that should guide us?
25. How does a person choose to view the world with hope?

Notes

Reflection/Ideas/Discussion

What scene during this segment of the film is most striking? Why?

26. Dialogue analysis: Birdee's mother tells Birdee that she has her own orange cones around her. What does she mean by this? Do you think young people in high school and college sometimes put up barriers around themselves? Why or why not?
27. Scene analysis: Birdee and Bernice argue. Given the circumstances, what do you think Birdee should have said to Bernice?
28. Scene analysis: Birdee chooses to get drunk. Obviously, alcohol does not solve Birdee's problems. Is drinking alcohol to solve a problem common in your locale? Why or why not?
29. Dialogue analysis: Ramona tells Birdee that "Mothers love their daughters even if they show it poorly." What is special about a mother's love for her daughter?
30. Dialogue analysis: Even though her dad does not completely understand, he says something significant about Birdee: "She's marked for happiness." What do you think it means to be marked for happiness?
31. Scene analysis: As Ramona talks to Bernice, director Forest Whitaker shows that Birdee has heard the same advice years before. What advice do you think Bernice needs? What advice do you think Birdee needs?
32. Dialogue/scene analysis: Bill and Birdee talk. In your opinion, who is most at fault in the conversation?
33. Scene analysis: Bernice wants to leave with Bill, her father. What is most striking about this scene? Why?
34. Scene analysis: Justin picks up Birdee and they go off in his car. What kind of preparation must Justin and Birdee make before they get married?
35. Dialogue analysis: Birdee says, "Childhood is what you spend the rest of your life trying to overcome." Do you agree with her? Why or why not?
36. Dialogue analysis: Birdee says: "Beginnings are scary. Endings are usually sad, but it's what's in the middle that counts the most. You need to remember that when you find yourself at the beginning. Just give hope a chance to float up. And it will." How have you seen this to be true in your life or in the lives of others?
37. Analysis: What can we learn from watching *Hope Floats*?

Notes

Meet Joe Black

General Theme

The most important thing for human beings to consider at their deaths is how well they have lived their lives.

SESSION I

From: Begins right away.
To: After Joe sees himself in a mirror and walks away.
Approximate time: 42 minutes

Theme: We all live with the certainty of death.
Scripture: Mark 9:30-32—Jesus foretells his death and resurrection.

Doctrine/Application

(Refer to the *Catechism of the Catholic Church*, paragraphs 1010-1014.)
What would you do if you knew that you were going to die within the next couple of days? Would you change the way you are doing things right now? Would you begin to treat others differently? Would you make an effort to pray a little more? Taking this question seriously can change the way we think.

In the movie *Meet Joe Black*, William "Bill" Parrish had to take this question seriously. The angel of death tells Bill that he is going to die. The angel decides to stay with Bill during the few days that he has to live, meeting his friends and associates and living with him. Thus, the movie takes the question a step further: What if a person was to live out his or her final days on earth with the constant reminder that death was imminent? Would that add further significance to a person's last days?

Jesus seemed to sense how his life would end. Moving from Galilee to Jerusalem, he saw what his actions would cause. "The Son of Man," he said, "is to be betrayed into human hands, and they will kill him, and three days after being killed, he will rise again" (Mark 9:31). Resigned to what he was doing, however, Jesus stayed on the road to Jerusalem, living with the thought of his death and resurrection. Jesus was certain of what he needed to do, and he let it guide his final days.

Preliminary Thought

1. What would most people do if they had the opportunity to know the hour of their death?
2. Name one accomplishment you want to achieve before you die.
3. From your reading of Scripture, how would you describe Jesus' idea of death?
4. Do you think that most people are prepared for death? Why or why not?

Notes

Reflection/Ideas/Discussion

What scene during this segment of the film is most striking? Why?

5. Scene analysis: Bill discusses love with Susan. What is the most important aspect of love between a man and a woman?
6. Scene analysis: Bill begins to experience a heart attack. Do you believe that most people take adequate care of their bodies? Why or why not?
7. Scene analysis: The young man at the coffee shop is killed. What were your thoughts during this scene?
8. Scene analysis: Bill encounters the angel of death. Does it scare you to know that many people will soon die? Why or why not?
9. Character analysis: Bill. At this point in the movie, how would you describe Bill's personality?

Notes

SESSION II

From: After Joe sees himself in a mirror and walks away.
To: After Susan and her father say "Good night" to each other, and Bill sighs heavily.
Approximate time: 43 minutes

Theme: Many things are more important than money.
Scripture: Matthew 6:24—People cannot serve God and money.

Doctrine/Application

(Refer to the *Catechism of the Catholic Church*, paragraph 2113.)
The Sermon on the Mount is a statement of Jesus' moral doctrine (Matthew 5-7). Gathering the majority of Jesus' practical theology into one place, Matthew recalls that Jesus had some thoughts about money. Jesus says, "You cannot serve God and wealth," warning that wealth can corrupt the human soul. In fact, there are several places in sacred Scripture in which Jesus warns his followers to be very cautious about material goods. Jesus knew that people who devoted their lives to gaining riches might forget about more important things.

In *Meet Joe Black*, Bill Parrish is a rich man. He had made his fortune and then, unexpectedly, he knew that he would die before he could really enjoy it. Suddenly, the angel of death reminded him that money cannot buy happiness. Bill begins to ask what has been truly important to him in his life. He immediately thinks of his family and of what his family has meant to him over the years. Recognizing the love that has been given to him, Bill approaches a true understanding of his life.

It may be easy for a rich man to live, but it is difficult for both rich and poor to die. The finality of death brings to light what is truly important. People who have generally spent their lives amassing riches have often given up the search for love of God and others. Concentrating on how much they have, they forget about who they are. A primary lesson of *Meet Joe Black* is that death comes to the rich and the poor. When death comes, wealth is not important.

Preliminary Thought

10. In your opinion, do Christians follow Jesus' teaching about money?
11. What should be most important in our lives?
12. The meditation tells us that in concentrating on how much they have, the rich often forget about who they are. What do you think this means? Do you think this statement is true? Why or why not?

Notes

Reflection/Ideas/Discussion

What scene during this segment of the film is most striking? Why?

13. Dialogue analysis: Joe and Susan talk about friendship. What are the most important qualities of a good friend?
14. Dialogue analysis: Bill tells Joe that "their business" involves only Bill. Do you think this is true? Why or why not?
15. Scene analysis: In the board meeting, Drew seems to be interested in money and power. Besides money and power, what seem to be the concerns of business world today? What concerns do you think business should address?
16. Dialogue/scene analysis: A woman talks to Joe about her pain. How do you feel about the use of modern medical technologies and medications to prolong the life of people close to death? For guidance, refer to paragraphs 2278 and 2279 of the *Catechism of the Catholic Church.*
17. Dialogue/scene analysis: Bill talks about his deceased wife. In your opinion, what is the best way to deal with the pain caused by the loss of a loved one?
18. Dialogue/scene analysis: Bill says that when he dies, he wants to leave something. How would you like to be remembered when you die?
19. Character analysis: Quince. How would you describe Quince's personality?
20. Dialogue/scene analysis: Bill tells his family that there is so much he wants to say to them. What do you think people should say to their families before they die?
21. Dialogue analysis: Susan says to Joe, "Men who never say anything about themselves are always married." Do you agree? Why or why not?

22. Scene analysis: Love begins to develop between Joe and Susan. What should be present in every beginning love relationship?

Notes

SESSION III

From: After Susan and Bill say "Good night" to each other, and Bill sighs heavily.
To: After Joe says to Bill, "Tomorrow, after the party."
Approximate time: 43 minutes

Theme: The highest form of love between man and woman involves total commitment.
Scripture: Mark 10:6-9—Jesus' teaching about marriage.

Doctrine/Application

(Refer to the *Catechism of the Catholic Church*, paragraphs 1646-1651.)
Besides being the story of the visit of the angel of death to Bill Parrish, *Meet Joe Black* is a unique love story. The angel of death, evidently some kind of heavenly being, has taken on the body of a human being. The angel-become-man seeks human love.

Christians should take exception to the way human love is expressed in most movies today. In love stories, a man and woman generally express their feelings for each other in sexual intercourse. *Meet Joe Black* is no exception. This is directly contrary to Christian doctrine. Jesus teaches that the physical act of love belongs in marriage: "...and the two shall become one flesh" (Mark 10:8). Making love should not be part of a relationship in which the partners are just beginning to discover their feelings for one another.

The development of love between man and woman must involve the idea of true commitment. If movies are to portray a true commitment, they must establish a very close relationship between the man and woman. Understood in that light, Joe and Susan express their love without total commitment to each other.

It is clear that in our society, the evil of premarital sex destroys relationships. It is also true that a love relationship without the proper commitment destroys lives.

Preliminary Thought

23. Why do Christians believe that premarital sex is a sin? In your opinion, are there times when premarital sex or extramarital sex is not a sin? Why or why not?
24. In your opinion, why do movies show the act of intercourse?
25. Do you think that most people who are building their love relationships have a true idea of what total commitment means? Why or why not?

26. Do you think that most people who are married have a true idea of what total commitment means? Why or why not?

Notes

Reflection/Ideas/Discussion

What scene during this segment of the film is most striking? Why?

27. Scene analysis: A secret board meeting is held. Do you think that this type of activity—meeting without the chairperson knowing about it—is wrong? Why or why not?
28. Character analysis: Allison. How would you describe Allison's character?
29. Scene analysis: A secret board meeting is held. Was Drew justified in what he did? Why or why not?
30. Dialogue analysis: Drew says, "It's life." What is he referring to? Is he correct? Why or why not?
31. Scene analysis: Susan and Joe make love. In your opinion, are scenes such as this detrimental to young people? Why or why not?
32. Scene analysis: Bill argues with Joe about what Joe is pursuing with Susan. Is Bill correct? Why or why not?
33. Scene analysis: Joe is with the woman in the hospital. What is the significance of the scene?
34. Dialogue/scene analysis: Joe tells Bill that his death will come after the party. Do you think it would be good for you to know the exact time of your death? Why or why not?

Notes

SESSION IV

From: After Susan and Bill say "Good night" to each other, and Bill sighs heavily.
To: End.
Approximate time: 48 minutes

Theme: Above all, human beings must love others.
Scripture: 1 John 4:7-12—God is love.

Doctrine/Application

(Refer to the *Catechism of the Catholic Church*, paragraph 2196.)
During this final segment of *Meet Joe Black*, Bill Parrish asks the angel of death whether he should be afraid. Death is not a happy topic. We fear how it will happen, and we fear what will happen after it. But we can assure ourselves of some relief from our fear: "Beloved, let us love one another, because love is from God; everyone who loves is born of God and knows God" (1 John 4:7). Loving others should take away the fear of dying.

In this final segment of the film, we encounter two examples of loving others. The first is Joe's love for Susan. Knowing the uniqueness of his love, Joe the angel is compelled to honor the human love in a specifically human way. The second example is Bill's love of others. Celebrating with people he truly loves, his birthday party takes on a very special meaning.

Both kinds of love are present in our lives. First, most people will embrace marriage. Those who do not choose marriage must deal with their sexuality in a loving way. Also, Jesus calls Christians to love everyone. If we want a healthy world, we must learn to love one another.

Preliminary Thought

35. Do you think that loving others can truly take away the fear of dying? Why or why not?
36. How would you define the "love of others"? How does the love between marriage partners fit into your definition? How do other forms of love fit into your definition?
37. In your opinion, do most people truly love their marriage partners all of their lives? Why or why not?
38. In your opinion, do most people truly love others? Why or why not?

Notes

Reflection/Ideas/Discussion

What scene during this segment of the film is most striking? Why?

39. Dialogue/scene analysis: Joe talks to Quince about love. Quince's definition of marital love is very good. He says, "[I know it is love] because she knows the worst thing about me, and it's okay. We know each other's secrets." What is your definition of marital love?
40. Dialogue analysis: Joe tells Quince to go directly to Bill and tell him the truth. In your opinion, are people generally truthful with one another? Why or why not?
41. Dialogue/scene analysis: Bill opens up to Allison. Do you think that fathers generally have "favorites" in the family? Why? Do you think mothers have "favorites" in the family? Why?
42. Dialogue/scene analysis: Joe tells Bill, "What I know is what I want, and there is nothing you can do about it." In what ways is this a selfish statement?

    Bill tells Joe that Susan must know who he is. Are people ever really able to know who another person is? Why or why not?
43. Scene analysis: Joe talks to Susan about who he is, and Susan gradually comes to understand. Joe is truly giving of himself in this scene. In general, do you feel that people in love truly give to one another? Why or why not?
44. Scene analysis: Bill and Joe show Drew's deceit. Money seems to be guiding Drew's actions. In your opinion, do we truly understand how large a part money plays in life? Give an example to support your answer.
45. Dialogue/scene analysis: Bill gives a speech. Undoubtedly for him, the fact that "we are all together" is most important. Also, he hugs and states his love for Allison and Susan. Love is his guide. In your opinion, do most people die in love with others? Why or why not?
46. Music analysis: Bill and Susan dance to the song, "What A Wonderful World." In what ways is our world "wonderful"? Give specific examples.
47. Dialogue/scene analysis: Bill and Joe express gratitude to each other. In your opinion, do we express our gratitude to others often enough? Why or why not?
48. Dialogue/scene analysis: To Bill's question of whether he should be afraid, Joe answers, "Not a man like you." What do you think Joe means?
49. Scene analysis: Joe comes back to Susan as the young man in the coffee shop, a character from the beginning of the film. What do you think this scene means?
50. Analysis: What is the most important message of *Meet Joe Black* for young people?

Notes

Patch Adams

General Theme

Truly caring for people is an important part of a physical cure.

SESSION I

From: Begins right away.
To: After Carin rides away on the bicycle and Patch acts like an angry cat.
Approximate time: 34 minutes

Theme: In order to heal people, we must pay attention to them.
Scripture: John 5:1-9—Jesus heals a man who has been sick for thirty-eight years.

Doctrine/Application

(Refer to the *Catechism of the Catholic Church*, paragraph 2196.)
Most of the healing miracles that Jesus worked in his lifetime were for people who came to him. He was always a kind healer who would not turn down anyone who came to him with faith. However, in the miracle described in John 5:1-9, Jesus approached a man directly. The man had been sick for thirty-eight years and had given up any hope of a cure. Jesus sensed the man's pain, went up to him, and cured him immediately.

Jesus was not a doctor, but he spent much of his life dealing with people who needed healing. His manner toward them was one of concern for their welfare, part of which involved a possible cure of their malady. The more important gift he gave them was his care for them.

The movie *Patch Adams* presents a true-life picture of a doctor who was concerned about his patients from a personal as well as a scientific point of view. Patch Adams is a doctor who is patient-friendly, a person whose story shows the importance of care and concern in a scientific profession.

We can learn much from Patch Adams. Many of us are or will be involved in a profession in which we will deal with people, whether working with them, helping them, or healing them. Dealing with people on a professional level is important, but reaching them on a personal level is just as important. When we recognize the dignity and value of others, we will work with them on a professional level while at the same time treating them as real people in need of love and care.

Preliminary Thought

1. In your opinion, what was the most important part of the healing miracle described in John 5:1-9?
2. In your experience, have you found medical doctors to be "caring"—people who want to help you as well as cure you? Explain your answer.
3. In what ways can young people show care and concern for the people they work with?

4. In your school or college right now, who are the people most in need of someone to care for them?

Notes

Reflection/Ideas/Discussion

What scene during this segment of the film is most atriking? Why?

5. Dialogue analysis: Patch says, “All of life is a coming home.” What do you think he means?
6. Scene analysis: This scene happens in the psychiatric ward. What do you think is the most challenging part of working in a psychiatric hospital? Why?
7. Scene analysis: Patch is speaking to the psychiatrist. Evidently, the psychiatrist is not totally interested in Patch’s words. Do you think most people truly listen to others? Why or why not?
8. Scene analysis: In a group session, the members of the group talk about the person with his hand up. Do you believe the group was making fun of him? Why or why not?
9. Dialogue analysis: Arthur says, “Never focus on the problem. See what no one else sees.” Why is this good advice?
10. Character analysis: Mitch. Do you think there are many medical students like Mitch? Why or why not?
11. Scene analysis: Patch connects with the old lady and with the meat packers. What does it mean to connect with others?
12. Character analysis: Bill Davis, the patient with pancreatic cancer. In your opinion, why is Bill so mean?
13. Scene analysis: Patch entertains the children in the ward. What did you find most striking about this scene?
14. Dialogue analysis: Dr. Walcott says, “Our way of doing things is the product of centuries of experience.” Why is experience good for an institution? Why is experience bad for an institution?
15. Dialogue analysis: Patch keeps telling everyone that they should be working with the patients. Do you agree with him? Why or why not?

Notes

SESSION II

From: After Carin rides away on the bicycle and Patch acts like an angry cat.
To: After Carin leaves and after the subtitle, "Medical School, third year."
Approximate time: 35 minutes

Theme: Even when a change means an improvement, there will always be people who want to do things as they have in the past.
Scripture: Luke 5:36-39—Jesus' stories about the new and old.

Doctrine/Application

(Refer to the *Catechism of the Catholic Church,* paragraphs 1961-1974.)
The professors of the medical school that Patch Adams attended were not prepared for anyone like Patch. He was irreverent, funny, unconventional, and most of all, he was doing things that had never been done by anyone in the past. Inevitably, Patch Adams came into conflict with the "old guard," the people who always depend on the past, distrusting anything new. A number of times during the movie, Patch comes up against statements like: "You do not understand what we have always done" and "Our way of doing things is the product of centuries of experience." Making humor and joy possible prescriptions for disease was not a tradition of past medical experience, and, therefore, Patch's mentors never considered the possibility.

Jesus had similar arguments with the leaders of his time. He was advocating something totally different from what the leaders thought important. Using the images of cloth and wine, he told the leaders that people usually have a difficult time accepting something new. Jesus' teaching put a different emphasis on some old laws and even introduced new laws. Jesus often encountered opposition, not because of his teaching itself, but because it was new and different.

We must have a healthy acceptance of the past. There have been many great accomplishments, and our lives have improved because of past acomplishments. But if we are to grow, we must be open to possible change. The past must give way to future possibilities.

Preliminary Thought

16. Do you agree that humor and joy may actually help the healing process? Why or why not?
17. What are some laws that Jesus re-interpreted or changed?
18. What are some elements of the past that had to change? What were some parts of the past that should not have changed?
19. What improvements do you think should be made to help humankind?

Notes

Reflection/Ideas/Discussion

What scene during this segment of the film is most striking? Why?

20. Dialogue analysis: Carin accuses Patch of never being serious. What are the disadvantages of always joking and having fun?
21. Character analysis: Dr. Walcott. Do you think the way he views life and medical education shows that he has a serious problem?
22. Dialogue analysis: Although you may not have any personal knowledge about this, what is your opinion of a rule that says medical students should not visit patients until their third year of medical school?
23. Dialogue/scene analysis: Mitch and Patch argue. Does Mitch have a legitimate complaint about Patch? Why or why not?
24. Scene analysis: Patch is with patient Bill Davis. Why do you think Patch's approach worked with Bill?
25. Scene analysis: Patch's "welcome" for the gynecologists was funny. But do you think it was too irreverent? Why or why not?
26. Dialogue analysis: People are complaining about the way they have been treated in hospitals. What would you change about health care?
27. Analysis: Patch describes a hospital of the future with "no titles and no bosses." Do you think this would be possible? Why or why not?

Notes

SESSION III

From: After Carin leaves and after the subtitle "Medical School, third year."
To: End.
Approximate time: 41 minutes

Theme: Highly motivated people are guided by a dream, even when they want to give up.
Scripture: Mark 14:32-42—Jesus' agony in Gethsemane.

Doctrine/Application
(Refer to the *Catechism of the Catholic Church*, paragraphs 702-706.)
It is characteristic of people who possess high ideals to be persistent. Even when everything seems out of focus, such people will be guided by their dreams. Never allowing hopelessness to rule, they let their ideals reign freely.

Jesus was willing to die for the success of his kingdom, but the mental pain involved was both unavoidable and overwhelming. Not desiring the pain, he asked his Father, "...remove this cup from me" (Mark 14:36). But he knew that what he was doing was correct and important for humankind. So he added his statement of acceptance, "...yet, not what I want, but what you want" (Mark 14:36).

In a similar way, Patch Adams allowed his dream to guide him. His dream of a free hospital directed him, but his path was not without pain. He began to understand that people could get hurt because of his dream. But his ideals were strong, and he was able to continue, allowing the thought of the good to lead him.

Both Jesus and Patch Adams teach us a valuable lesson. When Christians become convinced of what they must do, they cannot give up. There will be setbacks because it is not easy to allow love to govern one's life. But even though they may at times want to give up, Christians will always remember and follow their dreams as Jesus did.

Preliminary Thought

28. Give some examples of highly motivated people. Why do you think they are so strong in their beliefs?
29. It seems inconsistent that Jesus would be distressed and agitated and cry out in pain. What do you think is the primary lesson of Jesus' agony in Gethsemane?
30. Give some examples of experiences that people find painful, but that will be helpful in the long run?
31. What are some elements of pain that must be accepted if one truly accepts Christianity as a guide to life?

Notes

Reflection/Ideas/Discussion

What scene during this segment of the film is most striking? Why?

32. Scene analysis: Patch shows Carin the future site of the Gesundheit Institute. This is Patch's dream. What other incredible dreams have come true? Give specific examples.
33. Scene analysis: Carin shares with Patch the problem that she has had with men in the past. What can be done to help people whose past has blocked future growth?
34. Scene analysis: Truman and Patch steal supplies from the hospital. Do you think that this is morally correct? Why or why not?
35. Scene analysis: Carin is killed. What do you think Carin should have done before she went to Larry's home?
36. Scene analysis: Patch does not attend Carin's funeral as the others do. Why did Patch behave the way he did?

37. Scene analysis: We see Patch's immediate reaction after Carin's funeral. Given the nature of the undertaking, something like this could happen again. Could something other than the building of the Institute accomplish what Patch wanted?
38. Dialogue analysis: Patch prays. It is a typical prayer of people who have been hurt. Why do you think God permits pain in the world? What is the significance of the butterfly?
39. Dialogue analysis: Patch speaks to the medical board. What is most significant about the speech?
40. Dialogue analysis: Patch says, "Death is not the enemy; indifference is." What is the meaning of this statement?
41. Scene analysis: Patch graduates. How do you feel about Patch's behavior?
42. Analysis: What is the lesson that *Patch Adams* teaches?

Notes

Pleasantville

General Theme

We must deal with real life, and not hide behind what is fake.

SESSION I

From: Begins right away.
To: After Jennifer says to David, "Oh yeah, look at that," and a young lady is blowing colored bubble gum.
Approximate time: 40 minutes

Theme: When we live in a fake world, there is really no life at all.
Scripture: Matthew 23:27-28— Jesus challenges the scribes and Pharisees.

Doctrine/Application

(Refer to the *Catechism of the Catholic Church*, paragraphs 1905-1912.)
The *Catechism of the Catholic Church* tells us that the common good calls us to create the conditions that are necessary to allow people to reach their potential and goals in life. People must be free to make choices about what will guide them in the world.

In American society, we are free to choose what will guide us, but we often choose goals that leave us unfulfilled. In some instances, we choose something that is not in touch with reality. Jesus sensed that problem with the scribes and Pharisees when he told them that they were not dealing with the reality of their personal problems. "Woe to you, scribes and Pharisees, hypocrites!" he said. "For you are like whitewashed tombs, which on the outside look beautiful, but inside they are full of the bones of the dead and of all kinds of filth" (Matthew 23:27).

In the movie *Pleasantville*, the world of the television series "Pleasantville" was fake. Further, the series depicted life as if everything were just fine, with no difficulties and no crises. Even the crises were fake, solved with false answers, and always with the unlikely conclusion that everything worked out exactly the way the characters wanted. This fake view of life may not have been evil, but it was not real.

When we live in a fake world, there is no real life. We may think that everything is just fine, when in reality it is not. And in the end, we will discover that we can easily be hurt. We must accept the reality of life. Even though life itself is beautiful, there is evil in the world, and we ourselves are responsible for some of it. If we understand this, we can address the problems caused by evil; if we do not, we can never be part of the solution.

Preliminary Thought

1. What are the most important ways to show respect for another person?
2. There are many modern-day Pharisees, or hypocrites, in our world. Give examples of behavior that you consider hypocritcal.

3. Many television shows present false images of reality. In your opinion, what television shows present realistic pictures of life?
4. How do people show that they are fake?

Notes

Reflection/Ideas/Discussion

What scene during this segment of the film is most striking? Why?

5. Scene analysis: David's fantasy is of asking a girl for a date. What is the dating pattern in your area right now? Is it a good one? Why or why not?
6. Scene analysis: The bad news is presented to the students. Are young people affected by such presentations? Why or why not?
7. Scene analysis: David is watching "Pleasantville." Why do people appreciate shows like "Leave It to Beaver"?
8. Dialogue analysis: Jennifer is upset about being away from her high school because she was just beginning to be popular. Do you think the importance of being popular is stressed too much in high school? Why or why not?
9. Scene analysis: The young people of Pleasantville are in class. What is your definition of a good class?
10. Scene analysis: Jennifer talks to David about the way she looks, and David points out that the people in Pleasantville do not notice things like that. Why was the recognition of sexuality left out of the episodes of "Pleasantville"?
11. Scene analysis: Johnson cannot adjust to a different routine. Do you see this among adults or young people today? Why or why not?
12. Scene analysis: Jennifer and Skip "make out." This is an important part of the movie because it is only after this that director Gary Ross uses color. Do you think that sexual impropriety is a serious problem today? Why or why not?
13. Scene analysis: Skip sees color for the first time after his evening with Jennifer. The explanation of the use of color might be that a person becomes colored in Pleasantville when the feeling he or she is experiencing is real and not fake. Skip's feeling was real. Do you agree with this analysis? Why or why not?
14. Scene analysis: After Skip talks to his teammates, they all miss their shots. In your opinion, what is the explanation for this?

Notes

SESSION II

From: After Jennifer says to David, "Oh yeah, look at that," and a young lady is blowing colored bubble gum.
To: After Margaret looks out at the rain and says, "Cool."
Approximate time: 39 minutes

Theme: People discover true life only when they begin to feel honest emotions.
Scripture: John 4:16-19—Jesus speaks to the Samaritan woman.

Doctrine/Application

(Refer to the *Catechism of the Catholic Church*, paragraphs 1762-1770.)
Jesus' encounter with the Samaritan woman is important for many reasons. Perhaps the most important is that meeting Jesus was probably the beginning of the woman's conversion. Although the story does not say that the woman turned her life around, it hints at that fact. With her statement, "I have no husband," she acknowledges her sinful state. It might be said that she was honest about her emotions for the first time. As a result, she could experience life.

The use of color in *Pleasantville* is connected with a person's honest emotions. During this segment of the film, we begin to see more and more color. As the people in Pleasantville experience honest emotions, they gain color.

The primary emotion in life is love. Likewise, in the movie, the primary emotion is love. The discovery of love is presented in a sexual way as the young people first encounter it, but love must go much further than that. As David says to Jennifer during this segment of *Pleasantville*, "Maybe it's not just the sex."

The *Catechism of the Catholic Church* reminds us that emotions, or passions, are neither good nor evil. They move people to do either good or evil. If we want to be moral, it is essential that our emotions be honest, that we control our emotions and become people who contribute to the good of humankind. We can hurt people by allowing our emotions connected with sex, anger, or greed to control us. Our lives should be guided by honest motives that take into account the feelings of others.

Preliminary Thought

15. The meditation talks about the conversion of the Samaritan woman. What is essential for true conversion to a better way of life?
16. What are the strongest emotions that human beings have? How can these emotions be controlled?
17. The meditation says, "We can hurt people by allowing our emotions connected with sex, anger, or greed to control us." Do you agree? Why or why not?
18. In general, do you think that people today consider the feelings of others? Why or why not?

Notes

Reflection/Ideas/Discussion

What scene during this segment of the film is most striking? Why?

19. Dialogue analysis: David tells Johnson, "You can't always like what you do; sometimes you've got to do it because it's your job." Looking at the world of work, do you think most people like their jobs? Why or why not?
20. Scene analysis: Betty's cards change colors. Why did this happen?
21. Scene analysis: George and Betty prepare for bed. Sexual interaction has no place in Pleasantville. In contrast, some critics of our society say that sexual immorality is so rampant in our world that we never will be able to curb it. Do you agree? Why or why not?
22. Scene analysis: There is fire in the tree. What is the significance of this scene?
23. Scene analysis: The young man who asks David the questions appears in color. Why do you think he is colored?
24. Scene analysis: David opens up the minds of the young people by introducing them to books. Books express the real emotions of people, and, consequently, the books fill with material as the young people desire to read them. In your opinion, do people today read enough books? Why or why not?
25. Scene analysis: David places the black and white makeup on Betty. What is the significance of this scene?
26. Dialogue analysis: Jennifer complains to David that while she has had "ten times as much sex" as the girls in Pleasantville, she still appears in black and white. When David says, "Maybe it's not just the sex," what do you think he means?
27. Scene analysis: Margaret and David go to Lover's Lane. Why are Margaret and David the only ones in black and white?
28. Scene analysis: Margaret gives David the red apple, an obvious reference to Eve giving Adam fruit in the Book of Genesis. What is the significance of this scene?
29. Scene analysis: It begins to rain. Why do you think people in Pleasantville do not understand the rain?

Notes

SESSION III

From: After Margaret looks out at the rain and says, "Cool."
To: End.
Approximate time: 40 minutes

Theme: Discovering our honest emotions is both difficult and dangerous.
Scripture: Daniel 3:13-18—Shadrach, Meshach, and Abednego swear their allegiance to God no matter what happens.

Doctrine/Application

(Refer to the *Catechism of the Catholic Church,* paragraphs 1939-1942.)

Honest emotions are being experienced by the citizens of Pleasantville. But expressing honest emotions can easily lead to misunderstanding and sometimes hatred. This point is demonstrated by the people of Pleasantville, who were comfortable with their false existence. Suddenly, they face honest emotions. Some people angrily refuse to accept the new, honest feelings.

The three young men who disobeyed King Nebuchadnezzar's order did not desire to tear down a monarchy. They did not act out of anger at the king or hatred of the realm. They acted out of the honest emotions of good Hebrew men who simply would not disregard their God. Their action was difficult and dangerous, but they knew that they had to be honest with themselves.

Watching the conclusion of *Pleasantville* and considering the motivation of those who now appear in color, we are struck by how sincere they are. They had come to believe that to feel honest emotions was a good thing. In their minds, to be real is the only way to live.

We all need to understand the challenge of expressing honest emotions. Our emotions lead us to experience love, grow angry, feel the pain of others, or to be hurt by the actions of others. The three young men who faced torture by King Nebuchadnezzar and people who appeared in color in *Pleasantville* met the challenge of expressing their honest emotions.

Preliminary Thought

30. What are the strongest emotions that young people feel?
31. Do you believe that the honest emotions described by the meditation and *Pleasantville* always lead to good things for others? Why or why not?
32. What is the guide that most young people accept for expressing their emotions?

Notes

Reflection/Ideas/Discussion

What scene during this segment of this film is most striking? Why?

33. Dialogue/scene analysis: George says over and over, "Honey, I'm home. Where's my dinner?" What is the significance of his action?
34. Dialogue analysis: Big Bob says that there is a question of values. Do the people want to hold on to the values that made Pleasantville great? What do you think of his arguments?
35. Scene analysis: Johnson's shop. Why is Johnson's shop in color?
36. Scene analysis: Color is an issue in Pleasantville. How is the issue of color in Pleasantville similar to the issue of race in the United States in the 1960s?

37. Scene analysis: David finally appears in color. Why do you think it took so long for David to become colored?
38. Dialogue analysis: The code of conduct suggested by the Pleasantville Chamber of Commerce includes the following rules: "a) no public disruption; b) courteous treatment of each other; c) Lover's Lane and the library are closed; d) only certain music is allowed; e) no public sale of items for inclement weather; f) mattress measurements; g) the only colors allowed are black, white, or gray; h) a non-change-ist view of history." What is wrong with the code of conduct? What is right with the code?
39. Scene analysis: Johnson and David paint the wall with pictures of what has liberated them. What do you think liberates people?
40. Dialogue analysis: David explains to the court that the "coloreds" see something inside themselves. What do you think he means?
41. Scene analysis: Betty drops the mirror to David. What is the significance of the mirror?
42. Scene analysis: Jennifer decides to stay and go to college. What is the significance of her action?
43. Scene analysis: Betty is talking to both George and Johnson. What do you think this means?
44. Analysis: What message does *Pleasantville* have for us?

Notes

The Man in the Iron Mask

General Theme

In the end, good will overpower evil.

SESSION I

From: Begins right away.
To: After King Louis says to D'Artagnan, "Not if you find them first," and walks away.
Approximate time: 41 minutes

Theme: There is much evil under the disguise of what is good.
Scripture: John 11:45-53—Caiaphas speaks true words to cover evil motivation.

Doctrine/Application

(Refer to the *Catechism of the Catholic Church*, paragraphs 1755 and 1756.)
If one did not know the background of John 11:45-53, one might easily conclude that the decision of the Sanhedrin was both logical and righteous. If the Romans would come and take away the Hebrew land, the Sanhedrin would have cause to eliminate Jesus. If the whole nation would perish, "...it is better for you to have one man die for the people than to have the whole nation destroyed" (John 11:50). The problem, of course, was that the motivation of the Pharisees was not concern for the good of the nation, as they said. They wanted to satisfy their own selfish desires. They seemed on the surface to be working for the good of the whole nation, but, in truth, they were guided by evil intentions.

In the movie *The Man in the Iron Mask,* young King Louis XIV seemed to be a good king. He was not doing anything that would lead to war. He seemed to be interested in maintaining a good country. But under the guise that everything was fine, there was evil. The king had his own selfish desires. He did not care about the common people, who were suffering from famine and neglect.

We must all consider the motivation for our actions. Our intentions make our actions good or bad. We have the same problem as do the Pharisees and young King Louis XIV—we don't like to look at our real intentions. If we are true followers of Jesus, our actions should lead to good things, but that requires that our motivation be good as well.

Preliminary Thought

1. Why did the Pharisees want to eliminate Jesus?
2. Young people are often accused of being selfish. Do you think that most young people have selfish motives for their actions? Why or why not?
3. What are some examples of selfish motives that might be common among young people?

Notes

Reflection/Ideas/Discussion

What scene during this segment of the film is most striking? Why?

4. Scene analysis: The scene shows the prison. What is your opinion of the prison system in our country today?
5. Analysis: The movie shows that Porthos is a good, but crude, man. Why do people do crude things?
6. Dialogue analysis: Aramis tries to explain the importance of prayer to Porthos. Why do Christians stress prayer in their approach to spirituality? Do Christians pray enough? Why or why not?
7. Scene analysis: King Louis blames the problems of his country on the Jesuits. We often blame others when we should be blaming ourselves. Why do you think this is true?
8. Scene analysis: Raoul obeys the King. Obedience is very important in military circles and can easily be abused. Why is the virtue of obedience important for young people?
9. Scene analysis: King Louis makes love to a woman, but it is nothing more than selfish sexual gratification on his part. Do you agree with those who say that premarital sexual encounters are often merely selfish acts? Why or why not?
10. Scene analysis: King Louis does not listen when D'Artagnon tells him about the people who are starving. In your opinion, why did the King not listen?
11. Scene analysis: After making sure Raoul is no longer a suitor for Christine, King Louis courts Christine, eventually leading her to love-making. Throughout the scene, it is obvious that there is really no love on King Louis' part. In the dating patterns in your area, do you see people using other people as Louis was using Christine? Why or why not?
12. Scene analysis: D'Artagnon is loyal to the King. Do you believe that "The King, right or wrong" is an expression of true loyalty? Why or why not?

Notes

SESSION II

From: After King Louis says to D'Artagnan, "Not if you find them first," and walks away.
To: After Athos says to Philip, "These rooms are your mother's," and Philip replies, "My mother's."
Approximate time: 41 minutes

Theme: The greatest mystery of life is who we truly are.
Scripture: Mark 10:17-22—Jesus tells a rich man to think about who he is.

Doctrine/Application

(Refer to the *Catechism of the Catholic Church,* paragraphs 1700-1709.)

In this segment of *The Man in the Iron Mask,* Aramis, speaking to Philip, says, "The greatest mystery of life is who we truly are." He was speaking not only of Philip's identity, but of his character as well. Our identity includes physical characteristics, but who we truly are involves our character—the type of person we are or will eventually be.

During his ministry, Jesus gently led the people he encountered to a higher lifestyle, one that went beyond physical identity. Jesus invites the rich man to see who he truly is and to recognize what he must do. Unfortunately, the man does not accept Jesus' advice and goes away unhappy (Mark 10:17-22). One of the lamentable facts of human nature is that even when we know what will make us better or happier, we often refuse to do what we know we should. In effect, Jesus encounters each of us every day, telling us to look deeply within our beings, to see who we truly are and what we must do.

In this segment of *The Man in the Iron Mask,* we have the opportunity to witness the struggle of Philip and compare it to the struggle of the rich man. It is an excellent reminder to us to ask ourselves who we are.

Preliminary Thought

13. Spend a few moments in silence asking yourselves, What things are really important in my life? What are the characteristics that Jesus wants me to develop in my personality?
14. Why do you think the rich man could not accept Jesus' advice?
15. Do you think that people today are too concerned about the possessions in their lives? Why or why not?

Notes

Reflection/Ideas/Discussion

What scene during this segment of the film is most striking? Why?

16. Scene analysis: Philip has his mask removed. What would be the worst thing about wearing an iron mask for six years?
17. Analysis: Philip and Louis are twins, but their personalities are very different. Why do you think this is true?
18. Scene analysis: Philip is told that he has a chance to be king. If you were given a chance to be the leader of your nation, what would you want to change first?
19. Scene analysis: Even though it looks as if he can have anything he wants, Porthos tries to commit suicide. In your opinion, why did he feel the way he did?

20. Dialogue analysis: Philip is holding the mask. He says that he doesn't feel safe without it. What do you think he means?
21. Dialogue analysis: Athos, Porthos, and Aramis talk of the common dream that once was theirs—serving someone greater than themselves. What dream do you think Christians should have for the world?
22. Dialogue analysis: Louis lies about what he did with Raoul. Why is lying wrong?
23. Dialogue analysis: Louis says that he will not burn in hell since he is a king ordained by God. In your opinion, why do leaders often think of themselves as being above the rules that others must follow?

Notes

SESSION III

From: After Athos says to Philip, "These rooms are your mother's," and Philip replies, "My mother's."
To: End.
Approximate time: 43 minutes

Theme: God is directing everything toward the good.
Scripture: Genesis 1:31—God created only good things.

Doctrine/Application

(Refer to the *Catechism of the Catholic Church*, paragraphs 299-301.)

> Because creation comes forth from God's goodness, it shares in that goodness...for God willed creation as a gift addressed to man, an inheritance destined for and entrusted to him. On many occasions the Church has had to defend the goodness of creation, including that of the physical world.
>
> *Catechism of the Catholic Church*, paragraph 299

The Church has had to defend the goodness of creation because of the apparent evil in the world. Indeed, the evil often seems overpowering. How can the holocaust, for example, be something good, or the institution of slavery, or the misuse of power by a corrupt leader?

The believer has learned to look at the entire panorama rather than at a small snapshot. In this wide view, even the evils of the holocaust and slavery can be seen as stepping stones to a good future. In that same way, the musketeers of France learned to look past the corruption of an evil king to better days with a good king. They all believed that God directed everything toward the good.

A believer in God must always battle the problem of evil. It is essential for the believer to understand that it is God who has created the good, but that human beings create the evil. Once believers accept that, they will begin to see the possibility that the good will always win out because human beings can change the evil in their lives. Indeed God is always directing it to happen.

Preliminary Thought

24. What is the worst evil that has been present in the world? Why is this worse than all other evils?
25. How do you think it is possible to call the holocaust or slavery a stepping stone to a better future?
26. God is directing everything toward the good. What do you think this means?

Notes

Reflection/Ideas/Discussion

What scene during this segment of the film is most striking? Why?

27. Analysis: Do you think that D'Artagnon should have defended King Louis so strongly? Why or why not?
28. Scene analysis: Christine commits suicide. Why is suicide wrong?
    Suicide is common among young people. What can young people do to prevent suicide of other young people?
29. Scene analysis: The four musketeers and Philip come out of the battle alive.
    What is the motivation of people who give up their lives for some cause?
30. Scene analysis: The real King Louis XIV was the greatest ruler in France. What are the characteristics of a good ruler?
31. Analysis: King Louis grants his wicked brother a pardon. Why is forgiveness so important in Christian teaching?
32. Analysis: What message does *The Man in the Iron Mask* have for us?

Notes

The Rainmaker

General Theme

Mature people will always remain true to their convictions and beliefs.

SESSION I

From: Begins right away.
To: After Rudy says, "Sworn in by a fool, and vouched for by a scoundrel, I'm a lawyer at last."
Approximate time: 43 minutes

Theme: While Christians must follow the ethical standards of their chosen fields, they are called to go beyond simple professional concern.
Scripture: John 19:38-42—Jesus is buried by his friends.

Doctrine/Application

(Refer to the *Catechism of the Catholic Church,* paragraphs 1886-1889.)
Scripture does not tell us very much about Joseph of Arimathea or Nicodemus. The belief of most Scripture scholars is that they were professional people who had come to believe in Jesus. Although very cautious, they followed him, even to his death. Then, casting aside any previous caution, they boldly prepared his body for burial, an act of charity and a show of love and care for a person whom they had come to respect.

Rudy Baylor loved the law, and even though his family was not totally enamored with his choice, he had become a lawyer. Beginning his practice of law, he immediately started to see the problems and personal horrors of the people he was to help by being their lawyer. He knew what his professional ethics required him to do. He had the welfare of his clients at heart, but he felt he had to go further than that. His clients needed him not only as a professional, but also as a friend. Although he knew that he should not become involved in their personal lives—something he had learned in his professional schooling—he also understood the importance of the Christian virtue of caring.

No matter what way of life Christians choose, no matter what professional path they follow, there are certain obligations that arise. Professionally, Christians must follow the ethical standards of their chosen fields, but as Christians, they are called to go further than that. Christians are also called truly to care about the people they come to know. Sometimes it means going further than simple professional concern. Christian young people who are choosing their future careers must be aware that no matter what their future professional lives will entail, they will always be called to go further than professional caring.

Preliminary Thought

1. What is the difference between professional caring and Christian caring?
2. In general, do Christians seem to understand that they should care for one another?
3. If it is true that caring for others is a Christian virtue that must be studied and learned, what does that mean for young Christians in high school or college?

Notes

Reflection/Ideas/Discussion

What scene during this segment of the film is most striking? Why?

4. Dialogue analysis: Rudy's father did not like lawyers. Why do some people not like lawyers?
5. Scene analysis: Bruiser Stone is evidently a "crooked" lawyer. Do you think that there are many professionals who are evil? Why or why not?
6. Scene analysis: Donny Ray's father is an alcoholic. In your opinion, what would be the most difficult thing about living with an alcoholic? What could a young person do to help if either parent were an alcoholic?
7. Scene analysis: The lawyers are involved in "ambulance chasing." Do you think this is professionally acceptable? Morally correct? Why or why not?
8. Scene analysis: Kelly is a victim of abuse. If you discover that abuse is occurring in a family you know, what do you think you should do?
9. Analysis: Why couldn't Kelly just leave her husband?
10. Scene analysis: When Rudy lies to Miss Birdie's relatives, they start treating Miss Birdie differently. Do you think that people in general are this greedy for money? Why or why not?
11. Scene analysis: Rudy takes Donny Ray out for relaxation. As a professional, Rudy should not have done this. Do you agree? Why or why not? But as a Christian, Rudy should do whatever he can to show care and concern. Do you agree? Why or why not?

Notes

SESSION II

From: After Rudy says, "Sworn in by a fool, and vouched for by a scoundrel, I'm a lawyer at last."
To: Immediately after Rudy finishes with Mrs. Black, and the judge says, "Mr. Drummond," and Mr. Drummond answers, "Your Honor."
Approximate time: 44 minutes

Theme: It takes someone with courage to stand up against evil people who are in control of a situation.
Scripture: 1 Samuel 17:41-51—David fights Goliath.

Doctrine/Application

(Refer to the *Catechism of the Catholic Church*, paragraphs 1805 and 1808.)
Because of the well-known story in the Bible, many situations that involve a smaller person taking on a larger one have been compared to David and Goliath. Actually, the story involves more than most people understand. No one can rationally conclude that David could have won a battle against the Philistine giant. The writer of the first book of Samuel clearly sets up the story so that the only way David could have won was with the help of God. The reader of the story must conclude that no matter what the odds, evil can never win against God.

Rudy Baylor, the only licensed lawyer of the newly formed Baylor and Shiffler law firm, was a good man. He did not like to see rich women cheat their families; he could not watch a man beat up his wife. Most of all, he could not stand by idly while an insurance company killed a young man by refusing funding for an operation. He was a good man and God should have been on his side.

What seems to be true in the modern-day David and Goliath stories, however, is that Goliath usually celebrates a victory. An evil insurance company will not sit back and allow itself to lose money; an evil husband will not allow someone to help his wife. In modern-day David and Goliath stories, bad people win sometimes, and, although God and the good will ultimately win, it does not help in the present moment.

A follower of God will always win in the long run. But in the short run, even a courageous good person will have temporary losses. For example, their cause may seem hopeless to young people who really want to stop illegal drinking within their group. But evil can be crushed only by good people who have the courage to face the evil, no matter what the consequences.

Preliminary Thought

12. Name a modern-day example of the David and Goliath story.
13. In the modern-day stories of the struggle against evil, do you think that those on the side of good always recognize and accept the presence of God? Why or why not?
14. Do you agree that the good will always win in the long run? Why or why not?

Notes

Reflection/Ideas/Discussion

What scene during this segment of the film is most striking? Why?

15. Scene analysis: The insurance company offers a deal to the Blacks. Do you believe that this type of a solution happens very often? Why or why not? If it is possible, invite a lawyer to discuss this with your group.
16. Dialogue/scene analysis: Donny Ray chooses to fight the insurance company. Given the situation he was in, do you believe that it was the correct thing to do? Why or why not?
17. Dialogue analysis: Rudy talks about Donny Ray's courage. What examples of extraordinary courage can you think of?
18. Dialogue analysis: The judge tells Rudy that he is in "over his head." This is a true statement, but under the circumstances, this is probably the only thing that Rudy could have done. Give some examples of people who are in over their heads.
19. Dialogue analysis: Rudy comments that he hates the lawyers for what they represent. In the movie, the experienced lawyers seem to be evil. Do you think this image has a basis in fact? Why or why not?
20. Scene analysis: Donny Ray dies and Rudy attends the funeral. Donny Ray's father and Rudy communicate with one another. In your opinion, what is the significance of the scene?
21. Scene analysis: Rudy discredits the insurance company lawyers by using the phone tap to make them look ridiculous. Was the action in any way helpful to Rudy and the Blacks? Why or why not?
22. Scene analysis: Rudy evidently does not know how to try a case. Was there any other way he could have handled the situation? Why or why not?

Notes

SESSION III

From: Immediately after Rudy finishes with Mrs. Black, and the judge says, "Mr. Drummond," and Mr. Drummond answers, "Your Honor."
To: End.
Approximate time: 45 minutes

Theme: Sometimes the only way to help a situation may be to leave it, and help in some other way.
Scripture: Luke 19:1-10—Jesus calls Zacchaeus to a change of heart.

Doctrine/Application

(Refer to the *Catechism of the Catholic Church*, paragraphs 1427-1433.)
Perhaps Rudy Baylor could have been a good lawyer. Evidently, he still had much to learn, especially working within a court of law. But even if he could have been good in this profession, he had seen that the practice of law was not always a good profession. He observed how some lawyers used the law to their advantage. He saw firsthand how evidence that should have been admitted could be denied because of some technicality, and how evil men who committed criminal acts could legally go free. He had to conclude that sometimes a person might have to leave a profession in order to accomplish what he wanted.

We do not know from the Scriptures whether or not Zacchaeus actually left his job as tax collector. As he spoke of his repentance, it seems likely that he gave up his profession. But, whether or not he did, Zacchaeus made a drastic change in order to save himself.

Sometimes we find ourselves in a situation that should change because of some evil involved. We know it. Everyone who is part of the situation knows it. This may involve an organization as small as a service club in a high school or as large as a global insurance organization. When Christians discover evil, they must do something about it. Sometimes they may even have to quit the organization in order to work for change. But whether or not the Christian leaves the situation, a person who recognizes the evil must make some change—perhaps even a life-altering change—in order to work for good.

Preliminary Thought

23. Do you believe that a professional person could ever be morally obliged to leave a profession or a place of employment? Why?
24. In Rudy Baylor's situation, whether he wins or loses the case, could he do more good for the law profession by leaving it? Why?
25. Give an example of an evil situation in which the only moral alternative for those involved is to leave.

Notes

Reflection/Ideas/Discussion

What scene during this segment of the film is most striking? Why?

26. Scene analysis: Rudy Baylor is with Kelly and her husband. Obviously, Rudy should not have left the house, but he did. Did he have any moral obligation to report what really happened? Why or why not?
27. Dialogue/scene analysis: Jackie Lemancyzk explains the scam to Deck. Do you think there are insurance companies like this one operating in today's world? Why or why not?
28. Scene analysis: Deck gets a decision from Bruiser. In a sense, good is using evil in order to obtain information. Do you believe that Deck's actions were morally correct? Why or why not?
29. Scene analysis The Great Benefit Life Insurance company declares bankruptcy, and no one receives any money. What is your opinion of the legal action of bankruptcy?
30. Scene analysis: The bankruptcy declaration does not seem to be sufficient punishment for the people of Great Benefit Life Insurance. In your opinion, what other punishments should be given?
31. Scene analysis: Rudy Baylor leaves the law profession. Do you agree with his action? Why or why not?
32. Analysis: After watching *The Rainmaker*, what do think of the law profession? Why?

Notes

Titanic

General Theme

We are called to live our lives with sincerity and love, no matter what our circumstances.

SESSION I

From: Begins right away.
To: After Jack comes up behind Rose and says, "Don't do it."
Approximate time: 38 minutes

Theme: Material goods do not necessarily make people happy.
Scripture: Luke 12:22-31—God takes cares of his creatures.

Doctrine/Application

(Refer to the *Catechism of the Catholic Church*, paragraph 1723.)
The *Catechism of the Catholic Church* quotes John Henry Cardinal Newman on wealth. "All bow down before wealth," Cardinal Newman wrote. "Wealth is that to which the multitude of men pay an instinctive homage. They measure happiness by wealth; and by wealth they measure respectability....It is homage resulting from a profound faith...that with wealth they may do all things."

The movie *Titanic* begins by showing what it means to be wealthy. Cal Hockley was one of the richest men in the world, and he, along with his whole entourage, was accustomed to the finest accommodations, even aboard a new luxury ship. If one measured happiness by wealth, both he and his bride-to-be were bound to find happiness.

But Jesus tells us, "...do not worry about your life....Life is more than food, and the body more than clothing" (Luke 12:22-23). Jesus wants us to realize that God will provide for us.

Jesus' understanding of the importance of worldly goods is completely at odds with modern thought. Surrounded by materialism and commercialism that tell us getting what we want is important, we often think that satisfying ourselves with new and wonderful possessions will make us happy. We do not see a problem with this attitude and even consider having more goods the secret of good living. The truth is that material goods do not make us happy. In *Titanic*, Rose understood this fact. Many people must still learn it.

Preliminary Thought

1. Do you think that "All bow down before wealth"? Why or why not?
2. Do you think it would be a good thing to be extremely wealthy? Why or why not?
3. If you suddenly became very wealthy, what would you do first? Do you think this action would be selfish? Why or why not?
4. Many Christians are hypocritical with regard to wealth; they quote Jesus until they become wealthy, and then their outlook changes. Why does becoming wealthy often change a person's outlook?

Notes

Reflection/Ideas/Discussion

What scene during this segment of the film is most striking? Why?

5. Scene analysis: The search crafts and their crews look for the diamond. Immediately, we see that this portion of the film involves wealth. What other factors motivate the people who are looking for the diamond?
6. Analysis: The *Titanic* was supposed to be unsinkable. Why was this claim so important to the builders of the ship?
7. Scene analysis: Director James Cameron continually contrasts the inner workings of the engine room and the discomfort of the people shoveling coal there with the luxury of the ship. How did you feel when you witnessed these contrasts?
8. Scene analysis: Obviously in some way, Cal thinks he owns Rose. Do you see any way that Rose could have escaped the situation other than suicide? Why or why not?
9. Scene analysis: Rose is about to commit suicide. How do you feel about suicide as a solution to Rose's problems? Why is suicide wrong?

Notes

SESSION II

From: After Jack comes up behind Rose and says, "Don't do it."
To: After the captain says, "In fact, we're speeding up. I've just ordered the last boilers lit."
Approximate time: 38 minutes

Theme: Those who are rich and those who want to be rich often refuse to look inside themselves.
Scripture: Luke 16:19-31— Jesus tells the story of a rich man.

Doctrine/Application

(Refer to the *Catechism of the Catholic Church,* paragraphs 1723 and 2831.)
During this segment of *Titanic*, Rose tells Jack that he has a gift, that he "sees people." Seeing people involves having insight into who people really are and what they are really like. Usually,

people who have these insights about others can understand themselves as well, and recognize what life should mean for them. Jack, poor and without any roots, could do this; Rose, rich and with the tradition of her family behind her, could not.

Jesus tells the story of a rich man and a poor man named Lazarus. The rich man is clearly the villain. Refusing to take notice of anyone because he is so focused on himself, the rich man passes from life to eternal death. He did not recognize Lazarus' dignity and value; he did not recognize anything within himself that should have moved him to consider what he was doing (Luke 16:19-31) Perhaps his sin was in refusing to see who he really was, a person just like Lazarus. His wealth had taken over his thoughts. Because he had everything he needed, he did not feel that he had to think about his actions.

People who want to be rich are often infected with the same disease as those who are rich. They tend not to think about their actions and often look at others only from the point of view of what others can do for them. Christians would do well to pay attention to Jesus' story of the rich man and Lazarus. Riches can too easily block Christian thought and cause destruction.

Preliminary Thought

10. What does the gift of "seeing others" mean? What does the gift of "seeing ourselves" mean?
11. What do you find most striking about the story of Lazarus and the rich man? What do you think the story teaches modern people?
12. Do you agree that "People who want to be rich are often infected with the same disease as those who are rich." Why or why not? What name would you give this disease?
13. Do you think that most young people want to be wealthy? Why or why not?

Notes

Reflection/Ideas/Discussion

What scene during this segment of the film is most striking? Why?

14. Scene analysis: Jack talks Rose out of suicide. If you know someone is thinking of suicide, what is the best thing to do?
15. Scene analysis: Cal gives Rose the diamond and says, "Open your heart to me, Rose." He is trying to buy love. Do you think this is a common mistake of lovers in our world? Why or why not?
16. Scene analysis: The captain and builder of the ship talk about impressing people with the ship. What is the ultimate reason for wanting to impress people?

17. Scene analysis: The spitting incident. The director probably wanted to show Rose's desire to be a happy-go-lucky young person. In general, do you think young people are serious enough about life? Why or why not?
18. Dialogue analysis: Molly Brown calls the area of the ship in which the rich stay "the snake pit." Why?
19. Dialogue analysis: As Rose and Jack watch the rich people, Rose describes the evil actions that many of them are doing. Why do rich people often feel that they are not bound by any rules?
20. Dialogue analysis: Jack philosophizes at table, saying that we need to "make each day count." Why is that good advice?
21. Scene analysis: This scene contrasts the people traveling third-class who are drinking and dancing, with the people in first-class with their cigars and brandy. Describe the major differences between the two groups.
22. Scene analysis: Cal tells Rose that she will never behave like that again. There are many things wrong with the way Cal behaved. What was most reprehensible about how Cal treated Rose in this scene?
23. Scene analysis: Rose is with her mother. Her mother is interested in money and is intent on using Rose to get it. Do you believe that many parents use their sons and daughters to get what they want? Give examples to support your answer.
24. Scene analysis: The rich are attending the church service. What are the contradictions in this scene?

Notes

SESSION III

From: After the captain says, "In fact, we're speeding up. I've just ordered the last boilers lit."
To: After Lovejoy punches Jack and leaves.
Approximate time: 38 minutes (Allow time to change tape.)

Theme: When decisions are made, the consequences must be studied.
Scripture: Matthew 4:18-22—The apostles make the decision to follow Jesus.

Doctrine/Application

(Refer to the *Catechism of the Catholic Church*, paragraphs 1731-1738.)
People often make decisions without considering what the consequences will be. Therefore, there are many unplanned results of previous decisions. One of the signs of a person's maturity is careful consideration of all of the consequences of any major decision.

We do not know whether the apostles carefully considered their decision to follow Jesus. Matthew's gospel uses the word "immediately" to describe their acceptance of Jesus' invitation. If their decisions were made "immediately," without consulting family and friends, these probably were not the mature decisions they should have been. The apostles could never have imagined the results of following Jesus, of course, but it is a fact that the apostles gave up their lives because of their decisions.

In studying this segment of *Titanic*, we should take the time to consider all of the decisions that led to the tragedy. Before the ship was launched, someone did not correct the ship's inability to turn quickly. Someone also failed to understand the importance of having enough lifeboats for all the passengers and crew members. There was also a decision of sorts to accept the belief that the ship could never sink. These decisions were made long before the sighting of an iceberg. It seems that these decisions were made without a careful consideration of the consequences.

On another level, Rose tells Jack that she will leave the ship with him instead of with her family. This decision would have caused incredible adjustments for Rose. Decisions like this one, which have serious consequences, should be carefully considered. When a person chooses to marry, for example, or to make a lifestyle change, or to follow a direction that requires major adjustment, the person must measure the consequences of the choice. Reason, logic, and good sense can dictate our lives if we decide to allow them to guide us.

Preliminary Thought

25. What is the best way to prepare for a major decision?
26. Do you believe that Rose could easily adjust her lifestyle to Jack's? Why or why not?
27. Do you feel that, in general, young people prepare well enough for marriage? Why or why not?

Notes

Reflection/Ideas/Discussion

What scene during this segment of the film is most striking? Why?

28. Dialogue/scene analysis: Rose and Jack talk about Rose's situation. Although they both admit that ultimately it is up to Rose to do something about the situation, is there anything Jack could do to help? Why or why not?
29. Scene analysis: Rose poses in the nude. Do you believe that the brief scene of nudity has any effect on the young audience who may see it because the film is rated PG-13? In general, do you think teenagers between the ages thirteen and fifteen are affected in a bad way by the sex scenes in movies that are rated PG-13? Why or why not?
30. Scene analysis: Jack and Rose run from Lovejoy. The director shows the playfulness and the emotions of young love. Do you feel that the emotions of young lovers often overpower their reasoning? Why or why not?

31. Scene analysis: The ship hits the iceberg. Obviously, the captain should have been more careful. But who do you think was most at fault for this tragedy?
32. Scene analysis: Cal accuses Jack of stealing the diamond. Why did Rose not believe that Jack could have stolen it?
33. Scene analysis: After the captain realizes that the ship will sink, could he or anyone else have done anything to lessen the tragedy? Why or why not?
34. Scene analysis: The passengers pay no attention to the emergency. Should they have been informed in a better manner? Give examples to support your answer.
35. Scene analysis: The gates are locked, keeping the third-class passengers from coming to the deck. The action was obviously wrong. What should have been done?

Notes

SESSION IV

From: After Lovejoy punches Jack and leaves.
To: After the musicians stop playing for the second time, and one of them says, "Gentleman, it has been a pleasure playing with you tonight."
Approximate time: 37 minutes

Theme: True love is present when there is active concern for the other.
Scripture: Matthew 27:33-44—Jesus is crucified.

Doctrine/Application

(Refer to the *Catechism of the Catholic Church,* paragraphs 602-607.)
The *Catechism of the Catholic Church* explains Jesus' desire to redeem us. Jesus drank the cup that was given to him, a symbol of his active concern for those for whom he died.

> The desire to embrace his Father's plan of redeeming love inspired Jesus' whole life, for his redemptive passion was the very reason for his Incarnation. And so he asked, "And what shall I say? 'Father, save me from this hour'? No, for this purpose I have come to this hour." And again, "Shall I not drink the cup which the Father has given me?" From the cross, just before "It is finished," he said, "I thirst."
>
> *Catechism of the Catholic Church,* paragraph 607

Active concern for another is a characteristic of true love. People take care of those whom they truly love. Rose and Jack were proving that theirs was true love. They proved that they were actively concerned for each other, even in the face of death.

The death of Jesus is more than a good example for us. It is a statement of love that requires a response from us. If Jesus was willing to die for us, his message is one worthy of our full attention. We should have an active love for one another.

Preliminary Thought

36. In your opinion, what is the best way to explain the redemption that Jesus won for us?
37. Give an example of active concern for another that you have seen or experienced.
38. What are some of the obstacles to the existence of active love between all people?

Notes

Reflection/Ideas/Discussion

What scene during this segment of the film is most striking? Why?

39. Analysis: Throughout this segment of the film, people are making the choice of either getting into a lifeboat or staying on board the *Titanic*. What are the criteria that you would use if you had to make the choice for them?
40. Scene analysis: Rose helps Jack out of the handcuffs. This active concern is part of true love. How do you think married couples express this active concern for one another? How do you think the expression of active concern would be different for newly married couples, couples who have been married five to ten years, and couples who have been married over 20 years?
41. Scene analysis: Somebody had to make the decision to lock those traveling third-class in the lower decks. What do you think about this decision?
42. Dialogue analysis: Cal tells Jack, "I always win." Why do you think rich and powerful people often feel this way?
43. Scene analysis: Cal takes Lovejoy's gun and chases Jack and Rose. Why do you think he did this?
44. Scene analysis: Jack and Rose take the crying child, and a little later, Cal will use a child to get into a boat. What are the differences between the two actions?
45. Scene analysis: The ship attendant kills himself. For him, suicide seemed easier than suffering through the torments of dying on a sinking ship. There is evidence from history that others committed suicide aboard the *Titanic*. How do you think these suicides compare with suicides in general?
46. Scene analysis: The ship builder and captain go down with the ship. In your opinion, is this a good action? Why or why not?
47. Scene analysis: The musicians quit playing, but then begin playing again. What do you think this means?

Notes

SESSION V

From: After the musicians stop playing for the second time and one of them says, "Gentleman, it has been a pleasure playing with you tonight."
To: End.
Approximate time: 42 minutes

Theme: Commitment is real when there is complete giving of self.
Scripture: Matthew 27:45-50—Jesus dies for us.

Doctrine/Application

(Refer to the *Catechism of the Catholic Church*, paragraphs 612-618.)
The final segment of *Titanic* shows us that Jack and Rose have developed a deep and true love in the short time that they had known each other. Not only did the young couple show active concern for one another, but Jack gave of himself completely for Rose. Rose, reminiscing with the people who wanted her diamond, used the diamond as a final sign of her love for Jack.

As Christians think about true love of another, they naturally think of what Jesus did for us. We know that Jesus suffered and died on the cross because he wanted to redeem us. But these words cannot convey the pain and suffering that his decision meant for him. Nor do they explain very well the deep love that Jesus had for each of us personally. It was the supreme sacrifice of love that led Jesus to give himself up to the tortures of Roman cruelty. The supreme sacrifice was Jesus' way of saying, "I am committed to every one of you, forever."

Complete giving of self is not common in our world. People talk about commitment in friendship and marriage all the time. Carrying it out is something else. The courageous act of commitment that we have watched in the relationship of Jack and Rose in *Titanic* is an example of the complete giving of self, a guide to living out true love.

Preliminary Thought

48. What are some ways that a young person can "give of self" for another?
49. The permanent commitment that most people think of is the commitment of marriage. Why do you think we have a high divorce rate in our country today?
50. What are some other examples of permanent commitment?
51. Do you believe that most people really understand what Jesus did for us? Why or why not?
52. What do you think it means to say that living out commitment to others can save us?

Notes

Reflection/Ideas/Discussion

What scene during this segment of the film is most striking? Why?

53. Scene analysis: People are dying all around Jack and Rose. What effect do you think this would have on those who are still alive?
54. Analysis: Do you think seeing deaths such as those depicted in this scene from *Titanic* has an effect on young people? Why or why not?
55. Scene analysis: A priest is praying as the ship sinks. If you knew you were going to die within a few minutes, what would you do?
56. Scene analysis: The *Titanic* breaks in two and eventually sinks. The film has been praised because everything looks so real and is so believable. Do you think that films can be too explicit in portraying tragedy? Why or why not?
57. Scene analysis: The lifeboats have moved away from the *Titanic*. In one of them, Molly argues that they should go back for survivors. Someone responds by saying that they would be swamped if they did go back, and then everyone would die. What do you think of his argument? Why?
58. Scene analysis: Rose tells people about what happened. There were twenty lifeboats nearby and only one came back; only six people were saved from the water. Why did the lifeboats not go back for survivors?
59. Dialogue analysis: Rose tells of Cal's death. He killed himself during the financial crash of 1929. Suicides were common during this crisis. Why do you think this was true?
60. Dialogue analysis: Rose is talking about Jack. She says, "He saved me in every way that a person can be saved." What do you think this means? In what different ways do you think Jack saved Rose?
61. Scene analysis: Rose throws the diamond into the ocean. Do you think this action could be seen as Rose giving of herself for Jack? Why or why not?

62. Scene analysis: What is the significance of the closing scene?
63. Analysis: What lesson or lessons can be learned from *Titanic*?

Notes

Tomorrow Never Dies

General Theme

The desire for power is an evil that must be overcome if the world is to survive.

SESSION I

From: Begins right away.
To: After Bond hits the controller with the ashtray.
Approximate time: 37 minutes

Theme: Evil people will do anything for power.
Scripture: Matthew 23:1-7—Jesus warns his disciples about the scribes and Pharisees.

Doctrine/Application

(Refer to the *Catechism of the Catholic Church*, paragraphs 309-314.)
Jesus disliked the attitudes of the scribes and Pharisees. Jesus recognized that many of the religious leaders of the Hebrew people said one thing, but did another. Jesus warned his disciples, "...do whatever they teach you, and follow it; but do not do as they do, for they do not practice what they teach" (Matthew 23:3). Jesus also disliked their desire for show and ostentatious behavior. Exhibiting the type of behavior that gave them honor and fame, they sought power. Having the respect of others gave them a certain power that they used to their advantage. Judging from the words and actions that Jesus directed toward the scribes and Pharisees, a religious person must not behave as they did.

The movies that recall the fantastic adventures of James Bond, Agent 007 of English Intelligence, are filled with violence, sex, and power. *Tomorrow Never Dies* is no exception. The evil man Eliot Carver wants to become ruler of the entire world by establishing a global communications empire. He is hopelessly insane, but unfortunately the desire for power often does not diminish with insanity. In fact, in many instances, the unbridled desire for power causes insanity.

The use of power is a problem in our world. Many Christians succumb to its lure. In high schools and colleges, in political contests, and in day-to-day existence, people act out of a desire for power and control. Their desire for power may not cause people to desire to rule the world, but it can easily lead them to attempt to dominate in their home, in their group of friends, or in their work setting. Christians must be aware of the very human desire to control others. It can be a real evil in our world.

Preliminary Thought

1. In Matthew 23:1-7, do you believe that Jesus may have been too critical of the scribes and Pharisees? Why or why not?
2. What examples of modern-day scribes and Pharisees are you aware of? How do these people show the desire for power?
3. Do you think that movies such as *Tomorrow Never Dies,* which depict violence, are harmful to young people? Why or why not?

4. Why do you think the image of James Bond appeals to young people today?
5. In what ways do you see the desire for power in your high school or college?

Notes

Reflection/Ideas/Discussion

What scene during this segment of the film is most striking? Why?

6. Scene analysis: The scene takes place at the terrorist arms bazaar. What do you find most frightening about terrorism? Why?
7. Scene analysis: This scene, like others in the movie, involves killing. Do you think this type of portrayal of killing has an effect on young people? Why or why not?
8. Analysis: The movie shows the evil of a global communication network. What are the good elements that communication provides? Do you think that what we read in the newspapers or watch on television is for the most part true? Why or why not?
9. Scene analysis: Bond makes love to a girl. Do you believe that this type of scene is necessary to a movie? Why or why not? Do you see this scene as a put-down of women? Why or why not?
10. Dialogue analysis: The woman known as "M" tells Bond to use Mrs. Carver for information. What are some characteristics of using others that you see in high school and college?
11. Scene analysis: Carver tells the world in his first broadcast that he wants power to bring about good. Describe a type of power that you know has brought about good. Describe a type of power that has brought about evil.
12. Scene analysis: This scene, like others in the movie, involves fighting. Do you think that this type of obviously exaggerated violence effects young people? Why or why not?

Notes

SESSION II

From: After Bond hits the controller with the ashtray.
To: After Carver says, "There should just be enough time to watch it stop beating."
Approximate time: 37 minutes

Theme: If good people would confront evil people, we might be able to control evil.
Scripture: Luke 3:7-9—John the Baptist confronts the crowds about their lives.

Doctrine/Application

(Refer to the *Catechism of the Catholic Church,* paragraph 1808.)
What can one person do against the enormous evil of the world? How, for example, can one person contribute to preventing organized crime from taking over an area of a city? What can a person do to stop the bureaucracy that allows food to go to waste within a country of starving people? Is it possible for one good person to change an evil that many in the community accept?

No one person is able to make the impact that James Bond does. But the fantastic adventures of the English agent and his Chinese counterpart, Wai-Lin, in *Tomorrow Never Dies* can teach us something. Granted, both Bond and Wai-Lin probably would have been killed immediately if they were operating in the real world, but both of the agents did confront the evil. They risked their lives to stop an evil person from taking over the world.

This is an example of what courageous people have been doing since the beginning of time. John the Baptist, for example, knew that he was risking his life by confronting evil, but he also knew that the evil could destroy the world. He called the crowd a "brood of vipers." Then, he confronted their evil with words that stung: "...every tree...that does not bear good fruit is cut down and thrown into the fire" (Luke 3:9). John the Baptist challenged people to change their ways.

In the presence of enormous evil, one person generally cannot make a real difference. We cannot be a James Bond or Wai-Lin and completely eliminate the corruption in the world. But we are able to address the evil within ourselves. We can also do something about the evil of our own small community of friends or neighbors. Scripture and the movie challenge us to look at the evil that we are causing or the evil that we can do something about. Our small actions are part of the attack on the larger evils that are part of society.

Preliminary Thought

13. What do you think is the basic cause of some of the evil situations in our country?
14. What do you think is the worst evil in our world? Realistically, what can be done about it?

15. In your school right now, what do you consider evil? Discuss what individuals can do about this.
16. Ultimately, we must confront the evil that we do. What prevents us from doing it?

Notes

Reflection/Ideas/Discussion

What scene during this segment of the film is most striking? Why?

17. Scene analysis: Bond drinks alcohol. This is obviously part of the "macho" image of James Bond. Does seeing popular movie characters drinking alcohol affect the way young people think about drinking alcohol? Why or why not?
18. Scene analysis: Bond and Paris make love. Again, the macho image of James Bond is being stressed here. Do you think seeing this type of sexual behavior in films makes young people less appreciative of the fact that sexual intercourse belongs in marriage? Why or why not?
19. Dialogue analysis: Bond's friend says that Bond's desire to do something about evil is "an awful lot to save the world." What do you think you could do right now to "save the world"?
20. Scene analysis: Bond shows no fear. This is obviously exaggerated to fit the James Bond image. What do you think most young people are afraid of? Do you think that fear plays a large part in a young person's life? Why or why not?
21. Dialogue analysis: Bond calls Carver insane. Why do people follow the leadership of insane people like Carver in the movie, or like Hitler or other evil geniuses that have been part of our world?
22. Scene analysis: Carver shows the instruments of torture. Why is it wrong to torture people?

Notes

SESSION III

From: After Carver says, "There should just be enough time to watch it stop beating."
To: End.
Approximate time: 38 minutes

Theme: It takes courage to fight evil.
Scripture: John 19:16-19—Jesus courageously accepts his cross.

Doctrine/Application

(Refer to the *Catechism of the Catholic Church,* paragraphs 605-617.)
The theology of the Church concerning the death of Jesus on the cross is outlined well in the *Catechism of the Catholic Church*, which tells us that "The desire to embrace his Father's plan of redeeming love inspired Jesus' whole life, for his redemptive passion was the very reason for his Incarnation" (paragraph 607). Believers accept that Jesus died for them. This was the supreme sacrifice courageously embraced so that humankind could enjoy God's presence forever.

The salvation of humankind is the guiding motivation for the James Bond character. In *Tomorrow Never Dies*, James Bond and Wai-Lin courageously set out to thwart Elliot Carver's desire to rule the world. As Jesus of Nazareth came to bring eternal life, James Bond and Wai-Lin were trying to preserve earthly life. While Jesus' courageous sacrifice was infinitely more important, people who courageously fight evil on earth are also good examples for our lives.

During the last segment of the movie, we recognize that good people must confront the evil people of the world. It is profitable to concentrate on the courage that it takes to bring about the confrontation. None of us will ever be called upon to save the world like Jesus or James Bond and Wai-Lin, but we can study their examples to inspire us to battle courageously the evils that enter our lives.

Preliminary Thought

23. Jesus' redemptive plan was to save humankind. However, humankind must accept Jesus' plan in order to enjoy it. Do you believe that most Christian people act as if they have accepted Jesus' plan? Why or why not?
24. Define "courage," and give an example of a person who is showing courage at the present time.
25. It has been said that the world does not see real courage any more. Do you agree? Why or why not?

Notes

Reflection/Ideas/Discussion

What scene during this segment is most striking? Why?

26. Scene analysis: This scene shows an incredible motorcycle ride through Saigon. Do you think that anything like this could really happen? Why or why not?
27. Dialogue analysis: Wai-Lin tells Bond to kill Carver and that ultimately means Wai-Lin's death. Do you think that people are willing to sacrifice their lives for a common good? Why or why not?
28. Scene analysis: Carver shoots his control-man. Do you think that there are people so uncaring that they will kill simply to get their own way? Why or why not?
29. Scene analysis: Bond kills Carver. There is often some type of rejoicing when an evil person is killed. Do you think that we should rejoice this way over the death of another human being? Why or why not?
30. Analysis: What can be learned from *Tomorrow Never Dies*?

Notes

Index of Christian Themes in Films

CARE FOR OTHERS

COMMITMENT

CONVERSION

COURAGE

DATING AND MARRIAGE

EVIL AT WORK

FRIENDSHIP

GOD'S PRESENCE IN OUR LIVES

IMPROVING LIFE

INTEGRITY OF CHARACTER

MATURITY

PROBLEMS IN LIFE

Index of Scripture Passages Related to Films

Old Testament

New Testament

The Use of Rock Music in Ministry

Most Church ministers no longer listen to rock music; even many youth ministers have "mellowed out" with regard to their favorite music. But there is no doubt that we minister to youth in our parishes or schools who listen to some form of rock music—rap, heavy metal, or top forty. Consequently, a minister to youth must deal with rock music.

"Dealing with it" happens in many different forms. Many ministers dismiss rock music as evil, produced for the purpose of misleading youth. Consequently, they talk it down, condemn it, or simply ignore it. Other ministers substitute what has come to be known as "Christian rock," and try to interest the youth in the sound of rock that uses words with a Christian message. (I believe that Christian rock is good; it simply has not met my purposes.)

I propose that rock music can be used in a positive way. Almost any song that is released will have a message that is in touch with what young people experience or know about. To speak of rock music with a specifically Christian message in mind can be most effective for the Christian educator.

There is no doubt that the youth will know the music. Junior high and high school young people probably listen to two or three hours of rock music every day. The top ten are played over and over on the radio, so any song that is "hot" will be known, almost word for word. Young people practically live with stereophonic sound, whether in the car or in their rooms, and most often their choice of music will be some form of rock.

Rock music is an expression of an art form. As such, it is neither good nor bad. How it is used, of course, will constitute its morality. Entertainment is good, dancing is good, and background music is good. Indeed, looking at the words for positive expressions about life is good. Conversely, however, music used as a cult to Satan, as a "come on" to suicide or sex, or to prepare the psyche for drug use is bad. Most rock artists do not have good or bad side effects in mind as they sing and produce their music. Their bottom line, like the bottom line in any medium, is money. Anything that will bring more money—using outlandish makeup, bizarre behavior, or suggestive actions—is their concern.

Since the rock song is an expression of an art form, neither good nor bad, it can be used to accomplish one end or another. I believe rock music can be used for the good end of getting across a Christian message. Every song will have a definite message concerning life, and since Jesus and his followers dealt with life, I believe that Scripture can always be tied to the message of a song.

Therefore, Scripture plays an essential part in this book. Generally, however, the young person will not make the connection. Connecting a Scripture passage to a song is the job of the minister. My interest in writing this text is to make this job as easy as possible for the religion teacher, director of religious education, catechist, or youth minister.

First of all, before we get into the actual use of the rock meditations contained in this volume, here are some general guidelines for ministers who work with rock music. These come from the University of Hard Knocks—from mistakes I have made and mistakes I have seen others make as they attempted to use rock music with young people.

Incidentally, the comments that I have made about rock music also apply to country music. This volume contains some songs from the country charts since more and more young people are listening to country music. Also, country music often lends itself more easily to analysis than rock.

1. Generally speaking, young people know more about rock music than the minister does. Consequently, a minister must be accurate. Making up facts for the sake of a good argument only turns off youth, especially when the made-up facts hurt the reputation of an artist or group.
2. Most young people do not listen to all the words of every song. They will listen to recurring phrases and refrains, but many of the words are difficult for them to understand. But a religious educator must have a good idea of a song's meaning to use it in a discussion, even if all the words cannot be understood.
3. A little imagination can go a long way. In the rock meditations that I use, I sometimes stretch some meanings of the words to make an important point.
4. Generally, the best songs to use are current ones. Most songs will be taken from a CD that will top the charts for several weeks. In general, the young person must be familiar with the song if the minister is to make a point with it. The songs in this volume, and all of the songs in *The Message of Rock* series have been chosen because of their popularity. Also, I believe a very popular song can be used even if it is a couple of years old.
5. Prepare for the use of the song. If you play a song "cold," you will lack insight into the song and, because of that, you may miss a teachable moment. Combining the rock meditations in this book with the insight of the individual minister will achieve a very strong positive effect. Of course, those who work with young people can become so good at this that they can write their own meditations.
6. Be as professional as possible. Young people are accustomed to music played with professional quality: good sound equipment, beginning on cue, and so on.
7. Shortening the songs by only playing a portion of them or by talking over some of the closing verses can be effective, but ministers must watch that they do not ruin the song by talking too much.
8. The use of rock music and Scripture is only one means of enhancing a lesson. I believe it should be used often, but it can be overused. In general, use only two meditations during a presentation unless the presentation is on music.
9. I believe that the minister who uses rock music with young people will gain a certain insight into their music and may be able to use that insight to help parents. Parents often do not understand their young people's attraction to rock music, and a parish minister who uses rock music may be able to explain it to parents. Young people need advocates—adults who are willing to accept the responsibility of defending things that youth like. Rock music can be used in good ways and ministers who do it should be willing to explain this to parents.
10. Finally, the use of music described in this book will eventually give adults enormous insight into the minds of the young they are working with. This can have the effect of making these adults credible in young peoples' eyes. When that happens, then real teaching can happen. The minister will have an "in" with the young and be able to help shape the minds of today's young people.

How to Use These Rock Meditations

These meditations are designed for young people, grades eight through college. Any time young people gather for a religious purpose is a good time to use one or two of these meditations.

A word of caution concerning the use of a song and/or rock meditation in a parish setting—there is little doubt in my mind that all parishioners could get a message from the songs contained in this volume. However, given the fact that many older parishioners may be offended by the use of a song or by talking about a popular song in a liturgy, using rock music with the whole parish demands extreme care. Consult with and get approval from parish leadership.

These meditations can be used as discussion starters for high-school religion classes, classes in a parish religious education program, youth ministry gatherings, or college religion classes. The meditations can be followed by a period of silence, by using the discussion questions that are given with the meditation, or by using questions the minister may design.

Of course, the meditations may be used in any order. Young people may enjoy choosing which artist, group or song to use. It is effective to use all the songs listed under a theme on pages 124 and 125.

I find the following sequence most effective. Have young people spend a couple of moments of silence to center their thinking on what God wants of them. Then have a volunteer read the Scripture selection given in the rock meditation. After the Scripture reading, have an adult read the rock meditation. I believe that it is good for the young to hear an adult saying the name of the artist or group and the name of the song because this is an adult using the language of young people.

After reading the rock meditation, play the song. The song will generally be part of a CD. Often single cassettes or CD singles of the song are also available. I believe the cost of the music is money well spent from any budget. The minister may want to give away the tape or CD after its use, perhaps as a reward for participation. It is also very helpful to make the words of the song available. Usually, the words of the songs are printed on the promotional folder that is packaged with the CD. The words can also be legally obtained from the Internet.

Following the playing of the song and some possible introductory words by the minister, discussion can follow. Most ministers have developed their own style of conducting discussions suited to the age and size of the group. It might be worthwhile to make copies of the discussion questions so that everyone in the group can have them. Everyone does not need a copy of the rock meditation.

It is to be hoped that those who work with young people will become so proficient with the use of music that they will develop their own meditations based on current songs. The more contemporary the song used, the better. However, the songs in this volume have been chosen because of their popularity or the popularity of the artist or group, and should not lose much strength or popularity as they become older. For this volume, I have chosen songs with the strongest meaning from among those that were in the top five from October 1998 to August 1999.

Good luck! May the Spirit of God be with you as you make good use of popular music!

Angel

The Song: **"Angel"**
The Artist: Sarah McLachlan
Available on the CD: "Mirrorball"

Theme: We can find comfort when our world becomes difficult.
Scripture: Matthew 8:23-27—Jesus calms a storm at sea.

"There's always some reason to feel not good enough....I need some distraction or a beautiful release." The words of Sarah McLachlan's song "Angel" give evidence of the desire that so many of us have for some peace in our lives. "Let me be empty and weightless and maybe I'll find some peace tonight," she sings. "So tired....there's vultures and thieves at your back. The storm keeps on twisting, you keep on building the lies that make up for all that you lack."

The person in the song finds the peace "in the arms of the angel far away from here....You are pulled from the wreckage of your silent reverie. You're in the arms of the angel, may you find some comfort here." She finds her peace and comfort in the arms of someone who loves her.

Matthew's gospel also speaks of a sudden storm so fierce that it threw experienced fishermen into a state of panic. The apostles were being tossed and thrown in every direction, yet incredibly Jesus was sleeping through it all. They called to him in their fright, "Lord, save us! We are perishing!" (Matthew 8:25).

Like the person in Sarah McLachlan's song, the apostles find peace as Jesus calms the storm, saying, "Why are you afraid, you of little faith?" (Matthew 8:26). In effect he says to them, "You're in the arms of the angel, may you find some comfort here."

How do we define "angel," that is, the person or place in whom we find comfort and peace? *City of Angels,* the movie from which the song is taken, would define "angel" literally, as a real angel. But an "angel" might also be a person who helps others, or perhaps not a person at all. It could be that the place in which we find comfort and peace is a feeling or a belief or a ritual that soothes us when we are in need.

Christians have long believed that the person who calmed the storm on the Sea of Galilee for the apostles is the God who can calm all the troubles of life. It is good to be reminded of this from time to time.

Sarah McLachlan sings that the angel pulled her "from the wreckage of....silent reverie." We all seek such comfort. It is good news that we can indeed find it.

Discussion Questions

1. What are the most troublesome problems for young people today?
2. How do most young people find peace and comfort in the face of their problems?
3. What people or things are most comforting to young people today?
4. The meditation suggests that we find our comfort in the Lord. What does this mean in our world today? Be specific in your answer. Do you think that most young people would agree with you? Why or why not?
5. One way that the Lord comforts us is by bringing good out of evil. In what instances do you see good coming out of evil at the present time?
6. For those of you who have seen the movie *City of Angels,* can you give us examples of how the film shows the importance of using love as a guide for free will?

Notes

Back 2 Good

The Song: **"Back 2 Good"**
The Group: Matchbox 20
Available on the CD: "Yourself or Someone Like You"

Theme: Events of the past can hurt us so much that it is difficult to live in the present.
Scripture: Luke 21:25-28—Signs will indicate the second coming of Jesus.

Jesus knew about signs. Much of his ministry was spent trying to move people to read signs. It was evident when Jesus spoke of the second coming. There will be "signs in the sun, the moon, and the stars," Jesus says. "People will faint from fear and foreboding of what is coming upon the world, for the powers of the heavens will be shaken." But Jesus also says that there is no reason to fear since we will rejoice at being saved. He tells us, "...stand up and raise your heads, because your redemption is drawing near" (Luke 21:25-28).

If much of Jesus' ministry was spent in trying to move his listeners to read the signs of his time, much of our lives must be spent in paying attention to the signs around us. For young people, there are many signs, especially regarding love and building love relationships. The group Matchbox 20 calls attention to some of these signs in their song "Back 2 Good." They sing of people who cannot get things "back to good" because they did not heed signs in the past.

"Everyone here knows everyone here is thinking about somebody else," the group sings. "I couldn't tell if anyone here was feeling the way I do, but I'm lonely now, and I don't know how to get it back to good." The person in the song should have understood the signs of confusion, but did not. Instead, as the group sings, everyone here is "to blame, everyone here gets caught up in the pleasure of the pain, everyone hides shades of shame, but looking inside, we're the same...and we're all grown now, but we don't know how to get it back to good." Confusion reigns in the present lives of those who did not read the signs of chaos in the past. And "the good"— that is, how life should be—will suffer. In fact, the group ends the song with despair, "It's over now....There's no getting back to good."

One gets the impression that if the person singing had read and followed important signs earlier in life, then life would have been much better. It is important to understand that events of the past can make it difficult to live in the present.

Matchbox 20 sings of the signs of confusion; they sing of fake relationships and phony associations; they sing of loneliness and its effects. These are all signs that things are not as they should be, and if the signs are not heeded, "the good" will suffer. Young people—indeed, all people—must look seriously at their present activities, especially their interactions with others. At the same time, they should question themselves and "look inside" as the group suggests. Sensing the possibility of getting "caught up in the pleasure of the pain," people can work to control behaviors that are harmful, saving their futures while there is still time.

We do things in the present that can harm us in the future. Most of the time there are signs of such future harm if we are open to reading them.

Discussion Questions

1. Many Christians believe that we have the signs of Jesus' second coming around us. Do you believe that the end of the world is coming soon? Why or why not? For information on this, refer to the *Catechism of the Catholic Church*, articles 1042-1050.
2. What behaviors will adversely affect young people's future lives?
3. The song "Back 2 Good" in many ways seems like a song of despair, ending as it does, "There's no getting back to good." How do you define "despair"? Do you believe that people today are more inclined to despair than people in the past? Why or why not?
4. What are the principal areas of confusion in our world today?
5. The song mentions fake relationships and phony associations. What are the most important characteristics of good and true relationships?
6. The song uses the phrase "the pleasure of the pain." What do you think this phrase means?
7. What signs in our world tell us that we need to change?

Notes

Believe

The Song: **"Believe"**
The Artist: Cher
Available on the CD: "Believe"

Theme: After a breakup, one should not hold onto the past, but should begin again.
Scripture: Ephesians 2:1-10—We should be aware of the value of Jesus' pain and suffering.

Many rock and country songs are based on the inability of the person in the song to forget the past. It is especially true when a breakup has occurred, and the person does not want to let go of the relationship. Thinking that the future can never again be bright or happy, the person in pain holds on to the past relationship, even though it is over. The scene is repeated so often that this feeling of pain has been called the most common emotion that young people experience in high school or college.

In these cases, young people want to avoid what should happen. They should simply let the relationship die and move on with life. However, the emotions are often overwhelming since young people are feeling this pain for the first time in their lives. It is very easy for an adult or counselor to say, "Forget it and move on with life." It is very difficult for the young person to do this.

The person in Cher's song "Believe" had to make a choice that dealt with a separation. Feeling the pain of the moment, she is still able to overcome it. "What am I supposed to do," Cher sings, "sit around and wait for you? I can't do that. There's no turning back. I need to move on; I need love to feel strong 'cause I've had time to think it through, and maybe I'm too good for you." Her statement is interesting because she is looking at her pain in a philosophical way and justifying her action. In fact, she is worried about whether her ex-boyfriend can take the separation: "I really don't think you're strong enough now," she sings.

She must face the pain of separation. Many times in young lives, love relationships are temporary. These relationships will end, if not during high school, then after high school. If young people can learn to survive the pain of broken love relationships, their lives will be the better for it.

There are many places in Scripture that teach the value of pain. The Letter to the Ephesians tells us that we have been "made alive together with Christ...raised...up with him, and seated...with him in the heavenly places in Christ Jesus..." (Ephesians 2:5-6). Jesus' pain was the instrument of our salvation. Jesus teaches us that pain can be a way to improve ourselves.

A breakup can be seen in that light. The pain of a breakup might even be a treasure for the young couple, providing a certain loneliness that shakes the cobwebs loose in their minds and paves the way for other things to happen. The breakup can give young people time to get a little smarter and can bring them one step closer to knowing what they really want so they can seize it when it comes their way.

There is pain in a breakup, but as Jesus teaches us with his life, and as Cher points out in her song, there is "life after love."

Discussion Questions

1. The meditation mentions that the pain of a breakup is among the most common experiences of young people. What are some other painful situations that young people must endure in their lives?
2. If you have a friend who is suffering the pain of a breakup, what is the best thing you can do for him or her?
3. If you are trying to recover from a breakup, what can you do to help yourself?
4. What is the most common reason that early love relationships break up?
5. The meditation says that the pain of breakups can improve our lives. In what other situations does pain cause growth?
6. What do you think was most painful for Jesus in his life?
7. How can a breakup make a person a little smarter?
8. What does Cher mean when she sings, "Do you believe in life after love?"

Notes

Busy Man

The Song: **"Busy Man"** (This song is taken from the country charts.)
The Artist: Billy Ray Cyrus
Available on the CD: "Shot Full of Love"

Theme: We may be too busy to really enjoy our families.
Scripture: Ephesians 6:1-4—Some directives to children and parents.

A man dreams about going far in life. He wants success in his marriage, as a parent, and most of all, in his career. Now he has the perfect avenue. He has been offered the position of head of the psychology department.

But two things happen that influence him to turn the offer down. One involves his son, the other a visit to the cemetery. On his way out of the house on Saturday—he liked to get his paperwork done on a Saturday when no one was around—his son asked him to play basketball. He refused. But as he walked to his office, he passed the cemetery. Two questions hit him like a lightning bolt. Why am I working so hard? What is happening to the rest of my life when I spend time at work? At that moment, he changed his direction.

It may have been such an incident that inspired Billy Ray Cyrus' song "Busy Man." He tells of a man who wanted to go far, but had to neglect his wife and children in order to do it. Then the man thought, "Have you ever seen a headstone with these words, 'If only I had spent more time at work.'" At that moment, his life changed. "There's a call one day," he sings. "We need you down in Birmingham. You say, 'No way…I got plans with the kids and a day with my wife. I'm a busy man.'"

The song is a statement for parents. It tells them to spend time and communicate with their children during their growing years. This is an important song, calling our attention to the busyness that is detrimental to a family. The person in the song changes his whole attitude about life and decides to spend time with his family.

Divorce lawyers report that the second biggest cause of marriage breakdown is poor time management. The problem might be labeled "The American Work Ethic." Devoting themselves to work, husband and wife may be at work too long. Either one or the other may associate more with their colleagues at work than with each other. They may bring their work or the problems associated with their work home. One or the other may need to work two jobs. Soon spouses may discover that working can be much easier than communicating with family members. The family suffers.

Ephesians 6:1-4 tells children and parents how to treat one another "so that it may be well with you and you may live long on the earth." In the same way, if we could learn the lesson of Billy Ray Cyrus' song "Busy Man," we might be much happier.

Discussion Questions

1. Do you think people can achieve success in their marriages and families and at the same time experience success in their careers? Why or why not?
2. Why do you think people work so hard?
3. The meditation points out that Billy Ray Cyrus' song is a statement to parents about their work schedules. If you had the opportunity to say three important things to your parents, what would you say?
4. What are the best ways for teenagers to bring about good communication with their parents?
5. The person in the song changes his attitudes instantly. Do you think people can really change this quickly? Why or why not?
6. What do you think are the biggest problems connected with the work patterns of adults? What are the biggest problems connected with the work patterns of teens?
7. The meditation says that both parents and children suffer because of parents' dedication to work. How do the parents suffer? How do the children suffer?
8. If poor time management is one cause of the breakdown of marriages, what are some others?

Notes

Every Morning

The Song: **"Every Morning"**
The Group: Sugar Ray
Available on the CD: "14:59"

Theme: Achieving what we want physically does not necessarily guarantee happiness.
Scripture: Jude 5-7—A disciple of Jesus warns against sexual excess.

His life was not satisfying at all. In fact, he was thinking about that when there was a sudden slowdown of traffic. He swerved at the last moment, catching the fender of the car in front of him, causing only a slight accident, but an accident nonetheless. They managed to get the cars to the side of the road. The police were there, and then a priest showed up. Driving by, the priest had stopped to see if he could help.

The man who had the accident did not want to see that person dressed in black. He realized later that this was because of what seeing a priest did to his conscience. The man had been raised a Catholic, but had grown to disregard religion. In his mind, something he often told others, the Church did not understand anything sexual. Now, after having had affair after affair, he was in a relationship that he really wanted. But he knew that his partner was merely using him and, consequently, his life was not happy.

The sight of the priest brought his whole story to his mind and began some serious thought that ended with his return to the Church. He began to understand that ultimately his current relationship could not give him any fulfillment in life. With the help of a priest, he finally learned that trying to find happiness in sexual relationships was not going to make him the person that he wanted to be.

In "Every Morning," the group Sugar Ray seems to be saying the same thing. "Every morning, there's a halo hanging from the corner of my girlfriend's four-post bed," they sing. "I know it's not mine, but I'll see if I could use it....I couldn't understand how to work it out. Once again, as predicted, I left my broken heart open, and you ripped it out." He wants the relationship: "You know I wanna do it again." But it is also hurting him. "I never can believe what she said. Something's so deceivin'," they sing. The song does not tell us how the man resolves his dilemma, but one can easily surmise that the "halo" will grow into the "heartache" that he is already beginning to feel.

The disciple known as Jude knew that sexual overindulgence was wrong. "...Sodom and Gomorrah...which...indulged in sexual immorality and pursued unnatural lust, serve as an example by undergoing a punishment of eternal fire," (Jude 7).

Mature people know that they cannot find an understanding of life in sexual intimacy. Two bodies without minds can have sex. Animals do. But only people can "make love." The secret of being happy lies in striving to be a complete human person.

"Every Morning" is a song about the actions of many people in our society—those who seek casual sex and those caught in the confusion that results when immature people "use" others. Scripture calls for complete sexual intimacy only after marriage. This is good spiritual advice about the way to a fulfilled life.

Discussion Questions

1. Some people say that the Church places too much emphasis on sexual sins. Do you agree with the criticism? Why or why not?
2. Do you think there are many people in our society who try to find their happiness through sex? Why or why not?
3. What are the principal reasons why a sexual relationship does not always help a person?
4. Many people believe that "If we love each other, there is nothing wrong with having sex." What are the principal problems with this statement?
5. Why is premarital sex or extramarital sex wrong?
6. The meditation says, "The secret of being happy lies in striving to be a complete human person." What are the characteristics of a complete human person?
7. Why do many couples live together before they are married? Do you believe that this is always wrong? Why or why not?

Notes

Fly Away

The Song: **"Fly Away"**
The Artist: Lenny Kravitz
Available on the CD: "5"

Theme: At times, we all want to get away.
Scripture: Matthew 14:22-23—Jesus spends time in prayer with God.

The rangers who worked in the area knew that he was there, but they never knew why. He lived in a simple cabin in a canyon of the beautiful Ruby Mountains in Nevada. Coming into town only every other week or so, he was always polite and seemed to have enough money for his necessities. His constant companion was a friendly dog who listened well to his master.

He had never talked to anyone about his life, but when a newspaper reporter from the town asked, he was not reluctant to tell his story. The man had wanted to get away. He had been the CEO of a bank in Florida and simply had not enjoyed the world he lived in. He resigned his position, took his dog and his savings, and set out to live a simple life. Spending most of his day reading, he lived in his cabin with his dog and very few material goods. Remarking that some day he would probably go back because of his health needs, he explained that, for now, he was content to live the simple life he had chosen.

The banker accomplished what many people only wish they could. Stating the desire in various ways, many want to "get away from it all." In fact, airlines and luxury ships constantly entice their clientele with vacation packages that offer the complete getaway from life.

The message of Lenny Kravitz' Grammy Award-winning song "Fly Away" is the desire to get away. "I wish that I could fly into the sky, so very high, just like a dragonfly," he sings. "I'd fly above the trees, over the seas in all degrees to anywhere I please....Let's fade into the sun. Let your spirit fly where we are one just for a little fun." The person in the song wants to get away from the mad rush of the world.

Jesus wanted the same thing. Often during his ministry, he wanted to get away. Matthew tells us that Jesus "went up the mountain by himself to pray. When evening came, he was there alone" (Matthew 14:23). This is only one of several times when the evangelists recall Jesus' need to be alone. Time with his Father whom he loved was absolutely necessary for Jesus.

It is a well-documented fact that we live in a fast-paced world; it is likewise a fact that every self-help program mourns that we live in such a fast-paced world. Following the wisdom of people who have studied what our rushed world does to us, we realize that we must be able to slow down before we can begin to understand our lives. In fact, the proper use of our time might be the spiritual necessity of our modern age.

Spending time with God, spending time reflecting on Jesus' thoughts and words, will not slow the world. But it can help us to understand life and to live better, more fulfilled lives.

Discussion Questions

1. The meditation speaks of a man who leads a simple life. In your opinion, what are the characteristics of a simple life?
2. What are the main reasons why people in our world want to get away from it all?
3. Do young people also want to get away from it all? Why or why not?
4. In general, do young people like to be by themselves? Why or why not?
5. Why do you think Jesus needed to spend time with his Father?
6. What are the principal effects of the rushed world on people? Do you think that living in a fast-paced world has a significant effect on young people? Why or why not?
7. The meditation says that the proper use of time might be the spiritual necessity of our modern age. Do you agree? Why or why not?
8. Do you think that most Christians spend quality time reading Scripture? Why or why not?

Notes

Hands

The Song: **"Hands"**
The Artist: Jewel
Available on the CD: "Spirit"

Theme: If we rely on our faith, we will recognize what we can do.
Scripture: Luke 7:36-50—Jesus forgives and gives rest to a sinner.

Friends practically carried her home after she drank too much alcohol. Her mother was very angry. So, after she had slept off the effects, her indignant mother demanded an explanation, and an unpleasant fight ensued. During their disagreement, the high school junior told her mother exactly what was bothering her. "I feel stressed out most of the time," she said. "I'm not getting the grades that I should. I'll never get into a good college at this rate. Then at home I find a note from you saying to fix dinner because you're working late...again. Then my baby-sitting job canceled, and I really needed the money. I was ready to scream. I'm only sixteen, and if these are the best years of my life, I'd rather be dead. So, yeah, I went to the party and drank!"

This teenager wanted what Jewel sings about in her song "Hands." "If I could tell the world just one thing, it would be that we're all okay," she begins her song. The teenager in the story needed to hear those words. She wanted something that would make everything okay, take her away from her darkness so she would have no need to worry.

Where do we find such calm? Do we find it in the temporary relief of a substance such as alcohol or marijuana? Do we find it in suicide? Do we find it in a love relationship? Jewel's song presents no such answers. For her, the answer lies in faith. "I will gather myself around my faith," she sings, "for light does the darkness most fear."

Jesus encountered a sinful woman in search of calm. Anointing Jesus with oil, she put her faith in Jesus. Like the person in Jewel's song, she was depending on her faith (Luke 7:36-50).

But both the woman of the Gospel and the woman of the song present another aspect to this faith. They both understand that they have to act on their faith. The woman of the Gospel approached Jesus even though there were many who thought she was totally out of place. The person in Jewel's song understands that her "hands" are the means that she must use. "My hands are small, I know," she sings, "but they're not yours; they are my own...and I am never broken." That is to say, she will address the problem.

In fact, the person in Jewel's song goes even further. She understands that it is through her that God is working. "I will get down on my knees," she sings, "and I will pray....We are God's eyes, God's hands, God's mind, God's heart." "In the end," she sings, "only kindness matters," and the person who is to bring it about is God who is working directly through her hands.

Where do we find the answers to the emptiness of life? Ultimately, it must be in God. Jewel reminds us that we are God's hands in this life.

Discussion Questions

1. According to the story in the meditation, drinking alcohol is sometimes a symptom of stress. Do you think stress causes teenagers to turn to alcohol? Why or why not?
2. What are the principal causes of stress in young people's lives? Generally speaking, what are the effects of stress in a teenager's life?
3. What needs to happen in our world before we can become, in Jewel's words, "all okay"?
4. Do you believe that most young people possess the kind of faith that Jewel sings about in her song? Why or why not?
5. Name some ways in which you believe that God works through us. Be specific.
6. Jewel sings, "In the end, only kindness matters." Do you think that kindness is a virtue prominent among young people? Why or why not?
7. If the ultimate answer to the emptiness of life lies only with God, why do you think many people refuse to turn to God?

Notes

I Will Remember You

The Song: **"I Will Remember You"**
The Artist: Sarah McLachlan
Available on the CD: "Mirrorball"

Theme: We can learn from the past, but we have to live in the present.
Scripture: Matthew 19:16-22— Jesus encounters the rich young man.

He was an ordinary man in many respects. He had a job with the airlines, transferring luggage from planes to customers. He had a wife who loved him more than she should have, he thought. He had a child who probably would not grow up the way he wanted. Coming out of a program for alcoholism a second time after a failed first attempt, he was convinced that this time he would make it work.

Participating in his hospital-mandated therapy group, he told the others something that they all understood in one way or another. "You can't live in the past," he said. "I believe this is our problem. I liked what happened in the past too much and didn't want to let it go. I should have been learning from it instead of dwelling on it."

The recovering alcoholic's statement is quite similar to Sarah McLachlan's statement in her song "I Will Remember You." "Clinging to a past...doesn't let me choose," she sings. The person to whom she is clinging gave her everything, she sings, but now the person is gone. So she reflects, "I will remember you; will you remember me?" Meditating further on the past, she sings, "Don't let your life pass you by; weep not for the memories." She could easily feel the attraction of the past, but she knows that she has to deal with the present—without the presence of someone she loved—as difficult as it may be.

Whether the subject is love or life, dwelling on the past is not a way to maturity. The rich young man of Matthew's gospel was a person whose past had been profitable to the point of "having many possessions." When Jesus called him to further growth, asking him to give up the past he had loved, he was not able to do it. The young man was sad as he walked away from Jesus. For the time being, the young man had missed an opportunity to improve (Matthew 19:16-22).

People often miss the opportunity to improve because of their devotion to the past. In general, they do not want to let go of something that makes them comfortable, even when it is obvious that they should be choosing something or someone else. As in Matthew's story of the the rich young man, many people pass up the opportunity to gain real treasures because material possessions cloud their vision. In life, the pursuit of what is better is often hampered by clinging to what we already know.

There are many things that can be learned from the past, both good and bad. If we have made mistakes, we can learn from them. If we experience something good or beautiful, our lives will be richer. But to remain in the past often condemns us to solutions of the past. We must all learn to live in the present and allow the past to be a teacher rather than a dictator.

Discussion Questions

1. Is the consumption of alcohol by teenagers a problem in your locale? Why or why not? Why do you think alcohol consumption is such a large problem in our world today?
2. In what ways do you think living in the past can be a problem for love relationships? Please be specific.
3. If you have a friend who should let go of a relationship, what can you do for him or her?
4. Thinking of the story of the rich young man, do you believe that material possessions can prevent young people from achieving maturity? Why or why not?
5. In what areas in life do you feel the past can harm the present? Please be specific.
6. What are the most important things that young people need to learn in order to gain maturity?
7. In what ways do you think that the past can be a "dictator"?

Notes

Kiss Me

The Song: **"Kiss Me"**
The Group: Sixpence None the Richer
Available on the CD: "Sixpence None the Richer"

Theme: A couple discovering love for each other often show the love by kissing.
Scripture: John 2:1-11—Jesus and his disciples attend a wedding feast.

Her kiss had nothing to do with sex. She knew that he was in a very bad state of mind. She had called his sister who was a good friend of hers. Seniors in high school, she and his sister had come to do just about everything together. She had called the house often, of course, and when he, the younger brother, answered the phone that day, she sensed that something was wrong. He was a sophomore in the same high school that she and his sister attended. When he answered the phone and they had talked for a while, she knew that he had been crying. Quite naturally, she asked whether she could help, and he asked to meet her.

She listened to his story, immediately recognizing how close it was to the way she had felt a couple of years before. He told of his inability to express himself, especially to girls, of how he felt that he was not good enough for anyone, of how he thought that his parents demanded too much. She knew exactly what he was feeling. After two hours of talking, she leaned over to him and gently kissed him. It may have been the action that gave him hope to go on.

Obviously kisses happen in varying circumstances. Anyone who is beginning a love relationship soon discovers that kissing can be significant, but it also may mean nothing. Too often the action becomes nothing more than a come-on to immoral sexual play or a way to satisfy a selfish desire to feel better.

The sexual act of kissing is not mentioned in the New Testament. Jesus said nothing about acts that could lead to sexual intimacy. But he dealt with people who had shown love by kissing. According to Saint John, Jesus' first miracle was performed at a marriage celebration. From this, one could judge that Jesus' actions sanctified the various behaviors by which young people show their love for each other. One could surmise that Jesus might caution that such behaviors should be the sincere expression of genuine affection and appropriate to the level of commitment of the couple. But one might also surmise that Jesus would find sincere expressions of affection necessary.

The song "Kiss Me" by the Christian rock group Sixpence None the Richer is a song about kissing. The group sings the words of the woman in the love relationship: "Kiss me beneath the milky twilight. Lead me out on the moonlit floor....Silver moon's sparkling, so kiss me." The song tells us about a couple discovering their love for each other, and showing that love by kissing.

Books about Christian moral behavior contain very little material about kissing, but most of these books stress the importance of a couple's making a commitment. Physical actions should be a sign of real commitment between a couple. Therefore, a couple in love should know exactly what their kisses mean for them.

By his presence at their wedding, Jesus blessed the kiss of a newly married couple. For a Christian, therefore, a kiss should at least be the sincere expression of genuine affection. If it is, the discovery of love will be less difficult.

Discussion Questions

1. In your opinion, what are the most difficult things for a teenager to learn?
2. The meditation says that kissing often can lead to immoral activity between a couple. Do you agree? Why or why not?
3. It is a fact that drinking alcohol often leads to immoral sexual activity. Do you think that young people often drink alcohol with the desire to experience sexual pleasure? Why or why not?
4. The meditation says that Jesus would see the need for expressing affection. What guidelines do you think Jesus would give for kissing?
5. When do actions that are supposed to express love hurt people?
6. In general, do you believe that most of the physical actions between young people in high school or college are statements of sincere commitment between the two? Why or why not?
7. In general, do you believe that Jesus would be pleased with the way young people today display their affection for one another?
8. Why is the discovery of love so difficult for young people?

Notes

Livin' La Vida Loca

The Song: **"Livin' La Vida Loca"**
The Artist: Ricky Martin
Available on the CD: "Ricky Martin"

Theme: Some people will use others to get what they want.
Scripture: Judges 16:15-22—Delilah uses Samson's trust to get what she wants.

Although tragic, the story of Samson and Delilah is one of the most interesting stories in the Scriptures. It is a story of love and the abuse of love, of the weak and the powerful, of cowardice and courage. There is no better picture of the evil of using another than that of Delilah. Delilah wanted what she wanted. And what she wanted was money. With that on her mind, she set out to deceive Samson with what appeared to be love. Using Samson to pursue her desires, her actions were an example of the abuse of love.

Latin singer Ricky Martin's song "Livin' La Vida Loca" shows the abuse of love apparently for the same reason. "Woke up in New York City," the modern-day Samson sings, "in a funky cheap hotel. She took my heart and she took my money." "She" in the song resembles Delilah not only in her intention, but in her activity as well. "She'll make you...go dancing in the rain. She'll make you live the crazy life, and take away your pain. Like a bullet to your brain." His comparison is exaggeration, to be sure, but it is close to truth for the one in love.

It is an unfortunate fact that when people learn about love, they also learn about the abuse of love. There are many modern-day Delilah's and many people like the woman in Ricky Martin's song. In a love relationship, there are those who will use another to get what they want in the relationship. They will promise "forever," even to the point of marrying the other person, but they are guided by selfish motives. Like Delilah, they want what they want.

One of the difficulties in a beginning or continuing love relationship is the possibility that the couple may be using each other. It is especially true in relationships between young persons that often one or both parties do not even realize that they are in the relationship for the wrong reason. However, most of the time, with a little reflection, people can easily discern the sincerity of their partners. It is only a matter of time before the "real" person comes through in a relationship. People who only want the physical relationship or popularity and people who are merely acting will soon show their true intentions.

To conquer the evil of using another, the young lover must recognize the problem for what it is. Unfortunately, many achieve this too late in the relationship; that is, only after they have made some permanent decisions. Each person in the relationship must be inclined to break it off if one discovers that the other is using him or her. This is no easy task because often, even though one is using the other, both parties like the feeling of being in a relationship. Therefore, young people in love must take time to study their relationships.

When one person in a relationship is using the other, the relationship can never be good. The sooner young lovers learn this, the better their future lives will be.

Discussion Questions

1. In your opinion, what is most striking about the story of Samson and Delilah?
2. How would you define the phrase "the abuse of love"?
3. The meditation says that there are many people who are guided only by what they want. Do you agree? Why or why not?
4. The meditation says that with a little time, people can usually judge whether or not a person is sincere. How long do you think a couple should be dating seriously before marriage?
5. Using another in a relationship often comes in the form of sexual involvement. Do you believe there is too much premarital sexual activity among young people? Why or why not? Why is premarital sex wrong?
6. How do young people use each other in love relationships?
7. If a friend of yours is being used in a relationship, what is the best way to help him or her?

Notes

Lullaby

The Song: **"Lullaby"**
The Artist: Shawn Mullins
Available on the CD: "Soul's Core"

Theme: The most important characteristic to be fostered in today's world is true care for others.
Scripture: Matthew 8:5-13—Jesus heals a centurion's servant.

He knew the importance of military discipline, and he knew the importance of care for his men. But most of all, he knew the importance of being true to what he believed. If he felt something should be done, no matter what others thought, he would do it. And so, he was not ashamed to care for people, even slaves. To a Roman soldier, a slave was nothing—mere chattel to be used and thrown away. But this centurion was different. He was a man of his own principles, which dictated that he should care for others. Further, he understood that people should treat others with respect. So, when this wonder-worker Jesus said that he would come, the centurion told him, "Lord, I am not worthy to have you come under my roof; but only speak the word, and my servant will be healed" (Matthew 8:8).

Jesus praised the centurion, insulting the people of Israel who were observing him. "Truly I tell you," Jesus said, "in no one in Israel have I found such faith" (Matthew 8:10). Jesus healed the centurion's servant because Jesus cared about those who were suffering. At the same time, he rewarded a man who was bold enough to show genuine care for someone else.

Genuine care is the topic of Shawn Mullins' song "Lullaby." Shawn Mullins sings about a person who is trying to help a lonely girl. "From the stage," he sings, "I can tell that she...can't relax, and just before she hangs her head to cry, I sing to her a lullaby. I sing everything's gonna be alright." He tells her story: "She grew up with the children of the stars," he sings, and her parents threw parties and had important guests. But she felt lonely, and now, she is feeling safe in the bar. "She still lives with her mom outside the city, and...she's seen her share of devils in this angel town." He tells her that he's not so sure that the bar should be her home, but that "everything's gonna be alright."

The person in the song cared for the woman, and although we do not know what happened after he sang his lullaby, one could easily imagine that he was willing to follow through with his desire to care. The most important characteristic to be fostered in today's world is true care for others.

We all live with people who have seen their share of devils. Whether we live in Los Angeles, the city in the song, or any other city, there are many people who are in need of help. We simply must be more aware of the feelings and needs of others. A performer on stage can identify pain if he is attuned to the possibility; a high school student can recognize the discomfort of another student; parents can see anguish in their children; children can feel the distress of the adults around them. People can perceive the pain of others. We need people to care about that pain.

There are many lullabies waiting to be sung. It would be good for our world if we had people bold and caring enough to sing them.

Discussion Questions

1. We know that caring for others is an important characteristic that must be fostered in today's world. Name two or three other characteristics that a Christian should show toward all.
2. In general, people have a strong respect for the military just as the Romans did. How do you feel about the military strength of our country right now? Why?
3. Studying the story of the centurion in Matthew's gospel, describe the centurion's faith. Why did Jesus say that the centurion's faith was stronger than the faith of the people of Israel?
4. Recalling the girl's story in the song "Lullaby," why do you think she is lonely even though she has many privileges and opportunities?
5. Consider this phrase in Shawn Mullins' song: "She's seen her share of devils." What do you think the phrase means?
6. The meditation tells us: "People can perceive the pain of others. We need people to care about that pain." What are ways young people can show that they care about the pain of others?
7. What is the single most important thing that we should care about in our world right now?

Notes

Ordinary Life

The Song: **"Ordinary Life"** (This song can be found on the country charts.)
The Artist: Chad Brock
Available on the CD: "Chad Brock"

Theme: In our ordinary lives, we can recognize many extraordinary moments and opportunities.
Scripture: Luke 1:46-55—The Virgin Mary praises God with her ordinary life.

There have been many times in the history of our world when major changes have happened. When early man and woman discovered fire or the wheel, one can imagine people standing in awe and recognizing how great the discovery was and saying how good it was to be alive at that time in history. Or, in the present time, a person studying the incredible capabilities of a computer or the Internet could easily say how great it is to be alive now, even if the person feels that he or she is leading what might be called an ordinary life.

Country artist Chad Brock makes his debut with the song "Ordinary Life," in which he describes a person who becomes tired of what he calls the ordinary life. He has bigger dreams, and so he leaves his wife and son, and the doldrums of paying bills, going to Church, and going to work. "I feel like I'm trapped inside this ordinary life," he sings.

He begins to understand what he has done only after he has left his ordinary life. "I can't believe how much I'd miss," he sings after serious thought. "What I wouldn't give to pay the bills...go to Church, go to work. I can't tell you how much this hurts. I miss my son, I miss my wife, my ordinary life." He has begun to comprehend that the ordinary life is not so bad at all. In fact, he actually admires ordinary life and realizes how great it could be.

If we want to, we can teach ourselves to experience how extraordinary every moment is. When we do, we are looking beyond the ordinary life and discovering its deeper meaning. We are able to stand in awe and recognize how great it is to be part of what is happening, even if others call our lives ordinary.

The Virgin Mary lived an ordinary life, but she discovered from the start just how extraordinary her ordinary life could be. She received word that she would be the mother of the Messiah. Struck with the wonder of God, she prayed about how great her ordinary life was: "...the Mighty One has done great things for me.... and lifted up the lowly" (Luke 1:49, 52). She may have lived an ordinary life, but for her, living itself was an extraordinary event.

Without too much thought, we discover in history that even the extraordinary moments of the past happened in ordinary lives. Every moment becomes significant, a time to look beyond the ordinary lives that we lead, discovering that we are truly alive and capable of good, even great things.

Unquestionably, there are negatives. The person in Chad Brock's song sings that we can lose our perspective on life when we are overcome with the boredom of doing the same thing or suffering the pains of reality. There are negatives in any moment of history. But these can never overshadow the positives of the ordinary life lived with a mind truly open to possibilities.

There are extraordinary moments in history; and we may be living those moments every day in our so-called ordinary lives.

Discussion Questions

1. What recent world events have had the most significance for you? Why?
2. In the song "Ordinary Life," the person simply leaves his wife and his son. What do you think can be done to prevent families from breaking up?
3. The meditation says that if we want to, we can experience how extraordinary life is. In what ways are our ordinary lives really extraordinary? Be specific.
4. What is the greatest lesson that the Virgin Mary teaches us?
5. Given your individual circumstances right now, what extraordinary things can you accomplish?
6. The meditation refers to the negatives of life. What are the principal negatives that are present in our world today? Do you think a young person can do anything about these negatives? Why or why not?
7. If we really did consider our present life to be truly extraordinary, what effect would this attitude have on the way we live?
8. What are the best ways to improve our ordinary lives right now?

Notes

Save Tonight

The Song: "**Save Tonight**"
The Artist: Eagle-Eye Cherry
Available on the CD: "Desireless"

Theme: We must face reality with conviction, not with despair.
Scripture: Matthew 20:17-19— Jesus is determined to go to Jerusalem.

She considered herself a person who accepted things with a positive attitude. But she was witnessing a slaughter that her country seemed to be making no effort to stop. She simply could not sit back and watch because her strong Lutheran background would not allow it. What she was watching was wrong, and she felt the necessity to do something about it. With the help of friends who shared her views, she dug a basement below her house and sheltered Jewish refugees who were trying to escape from the Third Reich. They stayed there until the French Underground could get them passage out of Germany. She was an incredible woman who, at the age of sixty-five, gave life to hundreds of people. After the war a magazine interviewer asked why she, a Christian, had been so interested in Jews. She replied, "God doesn't distinguish race. It was incredible what was happening, but it was happening, and I had to do something about it."

Reality is often not very pretty, but it is reality and cannot be denied. What happens after we encounter reality is a matter of personal choice. Sometimes we may not want to do anything; sometimes we may not be able to do anything. But sometimes we can do something, and our action can be significant.

Eagle-Eye Cherry's song "Save Tonight" is not about saving lives, but it describes a situation that is significant for both people in the song. The man in the relationship must leave for some reason—that is the reality. He doesn't want to leave, and the woman doesn't want him to leave, but that is not the point. He sings, "You know I've got to go. Lord, I wish it wasn't so." It is important for both of them to accept reality. "Save tonight," he sings, "and fight the break of dawn. Come tomorrow, I'll be gone."

Jesus faced the reality of his death with conviction. Knowing what was going to happen, he did not give in to despair. Instead, he was forthright in his approach: "See, we are going up to Jerusalem, and the Son of Man will be handed over to the chief priests and scribes, and they will condemn him to death… and on the third day he will be raised" (Matthew 20:18-19). Jesus was resigned to the reality because he was aware of his mission.

Whether the reality is conquering the sin of the world or conquering the sin of a country or showing love and concern to another, we must accept the task with determination. People often try to hide the reality, or hide from the reality, never really accepting what is happening. Consequently, they cannot make the proper judgments, and they either lose control of themselves or lose sight of what is actually going on. People should never fear or avoid reality; they must accept it and deal with it.

We must operate in a world of reality. This may not be what we want to do, but it is the only way to live.

Discussion Questions

1. The meditation begins with a story from Germany in the 1940s. In your opinion, why didn't more Christians try to stop what was happening?
2. Looking at the reality of our world today, what are three or four areas that must be changed in order for us to have a better world? What do you think a young person could do to work for changes in these areas?
4. From your understanding of Matthew 20:17-19, do you think Jesus feared the death that he was about to suffer? Why or why not?
5. What are the principal reasons that people avoid reality?
6. Identify some situations in which people hide from reality? In each of these situations, what should be done to face reality?
7. If you see that something is wrong in your school or college, what are realistic ways to do something about it? If you see that something is wrong in your community, what are realistic ways to do something about it?

Notes

Slide

The Song: **"Slide"**
The Group: Goo Goo Dolls
Available on the CD: "Dizzy Up The Girl"

Theme: Young people about to be married should have the blessing of their parents.
Scripture: Mark 10:1-12—Jesus gives his teaching about divorce.

He had not wanted to come, but his friend had convinced him. It was a weekend meeting that the Church sponsored for people like him—people who had been through a divorce. He never thought that he would end up sharing his story, but during the first evening when everyone began to open up, he found himself revealing more than he ever thought possible.

He admitted that his life was a mess, but he called the beginning of his marriage the "real mess." Caught up in the emotion of the moment, he and his future spouse embraced the whole spectrum of what he described as "playing house." During their final year of college, the couple lived together. When his girlfriend became pregnant, they decided to marry. Both sets of parents were against the marriage because they felt that the young couple had not known one another long enough, but he and his fiancée were caught up in the euphoria of the moment. Neither could believe the hostile feelings that soon developed, causing them literally to hate each other. He felt that there was no hope for happiness for him because he now hated the only person that he had loved.

The weekend was a good experience, but it would take many years before he could understand exactly what had happened to him.

Jesus' teaching on divorce does not mention anything about preparation for marriage. He only says, "Therefore what God has joined together, let no one separate" (Mark 10:9). It stands to reason, however, that given such a difficult teaching, there must be some type of preparation. Perhaps during the questioning session that his disciples conducted in the house, Jesus was more explicit about the ways to plan for the complex task of living together and raising a healthy family.

Whether or not Jesus actually gave a teaching about marriage preparation, it may be the single most important part of the marriage covenant in modern society. Because casual relationships often blossom into marriage without serious thought by the partners, young people need to look objectively at their relationships.

The song by the Goo Goo Dolls called "Slide" is a perfect example of the casual approach of so many lovers. "I wanna wake up where you are, so why don't you slide?" To him, that is. But such sliding has consequences. He talks of the problems, even though he does not recognize them as obstacles: "The priest is on the phone; your father hit the wall; your ma disowned you. Don't suppose I'll ever know what it means to be a man." He is overcome by the emotion of the moment: "I'll do anything you ever dreamed to be complete....Put your arms around me....Do you wanna get married, or run away?" Emotion had prepared him for the single most important decision in his life. And since emotion is usually not good preparation, he paid the consequences.

Young people today are growing up in highly complicated times. The media, their feelings, and even their family backgrounds often direct them to pursue an emotional relationship that has no foundation. Guided by parents and reason, they can understand what their future might be. But perhaps most important of all, they must allow themselves some time of intense preparation before they embark on marriage or other life-changing undertakings.

Discussion Questions

1. In your opinion, what is the most difficult problem caused by divorce?
2. The meditation mentions young people living together before marriage. Do you believe that this is good preparation for marriage? Why or why not? Why do you suppose statistics show that living together is not good preparation for marriage?
3. Jesus' teaching on divorce is very clear. Why do you think there so many Christians— followers of Jesus—who go against his teaching in this matter?
4. The meditation refers to the need for preparation for marriage. In your opinion, what elements should be considered when a couple is preparing for marriage?
5. Why is emotional love alone a poor preparation for marriage?
6. The meditation tells us that parents play an important part in preparation for marriage. Do you agree? Why or why not?
7. Invite a couple who is involved in "Engaged Encounter" to explain to you what happens during this preparation weekend.

Notes

Somebody's Out There Watching

The Song: **"Somebody's Out There Watching"** (This song can be found on the country charts.)
The Group: The Kinleys
Available on the CD single: "Somebody's Out There Watching"

Theme: Our belief in God must be real.
Scripture: Matthew 6:30-33—Jesus tells us that God will take care of us.

Sitting down to reason it out, he knew that he should not have been alive. No one, he reflected, can crash-land a private plane in the mountains of Alaska, suffer through a snowstorm, and come back to tell of it. During his agony, he remembered seeing a happy, young girl—a girl who resembled his sister who had died years earlier from leukemia. The girl had told him to hold on, that she was watching over him, and that help would come. Help did come, and the tragedy that could have been never happened.

The man told his story often and was proud that the ordeal in the mountains had made him what he called a "real believer." In his lecture, he mentioned that he had always believed in God, but without conviction. Now, he said, he knew that God was real and had intervened in his life.

Jesus knew that God was real and would always intervene in people's lives. He told those gathered for the Sermon on the Mount, "...if God so clothes the grass of the field, which is alive today and tomorrow is thrown into the oven, will he not much more clothe you—you of little faith?....all these things will be given to you as well" (Matthew 6:30-33). In Jesus' mind, God always cares for us.

Sometimes, the music industry says the same thing. Even though today's music is created with the thought of making money, every once in a while a song is produced which is an unabashed statement of belief in God. This is the nature of "Somebody's Out There Watching," the song by the country music group, the Kinleys. "Hidden from us," the Kinleys sing, "in the sky above us, I can feel it all around; hard to see it, but I do believe that there are angels looking down....I believe somebody's out there watchin' over me." The song not only acknowledges the presence of angels, but also acknowledges the presence of somebody (God) who watches out for us. In the song this Somebody is responsible for the hope, truth, and dreams which are necessary to give "some kind of peace of mind."

Unfortunately, the peace of mind that the Kinleys sing about is not the same peace of mind that the world is looking for. The peace that the world desires is often defined in terms of power, control, and monetary advancement. It is no wonder that there is a feeling that God no longer cares for us. We want what God does not desire to give.

We live in a world where illegitimate birth rates are high, and yet over half of us do not even think this is a moral problem. Over fifty percent of our permanent commitments to each other do not turn out to be permanent. We pray for personal help from God, but less than half of us attend Church or a religious service every week, and well over half of us spend up to a quarter of every day watching television programming that often ridicules traditional moral values. We may say that we believe in God, but many of us are not acting like we do.

We need statements of belief like the Kinleys make in their song "Somebody's Out There Watching," but we also need to know what belief in God really means.

Discussion Questions

1. Do you believe that visions like the one described in the story in the meditation really happen? Why or why not?
2. Do you think that there are many people today who do not believe in God? Why or why not? Explain what belief without conviction means.
3 Christians believe that God really cares for us. But then how do Christians explain the fact that there are thousands of people suffering in our world?
4. In your opinion, what is the best proof that God exists?
5. The meditation tells us, "We want what God does not desire to give." Do you agree? Why or why not?
6. Why are illegitimate births, divorces, and uncontrolled television viewing moral problems?
7. What are the characteristics of real belief in God?

Notes

Thank U

The Song: **"Thank U"**
The Artist: Alanis Morissette
Available on the CD: "Supposed Former Infatuation Junkie"

Theme: When people finally slow down long enough to think seriously, they can change for the better.
Scripture: Mark 1:2-5—John the Baptist baptizes in the Jordan river.

Her job was to cover NFL games in the city in which she lived. As a consequence, during the fall and winter seasons, she had little time to spend by herself and with her young daughter. Being a single mother, she knew that her daughter was suffering, but she did not know how to manage her time better.

When she was assigned to do a profile of one of the linebackers on the team, she had no idea it would have the effect that it did. The linebacker was a unique young man with a wife and one child. Although his passion was football, his love was his family. As she interviewed him, she discovered what the linebacker called his "secret of time." He was busy with football, but he always carefully planned his day so that when he was at home, he could spend quality time with his family.

But what was even more impressive to the television reporter was the linebacker's devotion to personal meditation. Part of his "secret of time," he explained to her, was a fifteen-minute period of silence and meditation each day. He told the reporter that the time he spent with God was more important to him than football, and that it was this time spent with God that helped him to love his family and control his life. In fact, the television reporter vividly remembered seeing him on the bench before and sometimes during a game with his head bowed and his hands resting on his knees. The interview changed her life, and now she too extolls the value of meditation in controlling one's life. She deliberately spends more time by herself and with her daughter.

Alanis Morissette agrees in her song "Thank U." "The moment I let go of it was… the moment I touched down," she sings. And so, she thanks everyone and everything that had anything to do with her conversion. "Thank you, terror, disillusionment, frailty, providence, nothingness, clarity," and especially, she says, "Thank you, silence." In an interview, she explained that "I had never stopped in my whole life, hadn't taken a long breath. I took a year and a half off and basically learned to do that. When I did stop and I was silent and ready to deal with things, I was left with an immense amount of gratitude and inspiration."

The pattern of busyness leading us to forget the important things in life is common in our world. It was common even in the world of John the Baptist. Somehow his preaching had struck a chord in the hearts of the men and women who sensed that their lives should have had more meaning. They listened to him proclaim "a baptism of repentance for the forgiveness of sins" and they were being baptized "in the river Jordan, confessing their sins" (Mark 1:4-5).

The people of our world who are constantly too busy should learn a lesson from people who have deliberately accepted some regimentation into their lives. John the Baptist imposed a rule of life on himself and his followers by external washing. Alanis Morissette forced herself to take some time away. Led by such examples, we should see what our busyness can do to us and make efforts to slow down and change for the better.

Discussion Questions

1. As you learn about the high-profile lives that people like professional football players or popular singers have, what do you think are the principal drawbacks for them when they try to lead good lives? How can such a person manage to live a good life?
2. The story in the meditation deals with a person who spends time every day in silence with his God. What do you think a person should think about during a daily meditation with God?
3. Why do you think Alanis Morissette thanks negative things like terror, frailty, and nothingness?
4. Why did John the Baptist have such an impact on people?
5. What lesson do you think a busy high school or college student can learn from Alanis Morissette's song "Thank U"?
6. The meditation mentions a need for people to take control of their lives. Identify two or three areas in which young people should try to control their lives.
7. What two or three things need to happen if we want to live fulfilled lives?

Notes

Index of Christian Themes in Songs

BEGINNING LOVE RELATIONSHIPS

BUILDING LOVE RELATIONSHIPS

CHANGING BEHAVIOR

FAITH IN GOD AND JESUS

THE CHRISTIAN AND THE WORLD

YOUNG PEOPLE AND THEIR PARENTS

Index of Scripture Passages Related to Songs

OLD TESTAMENT

NEW TESTAMENT

Index of Artists and Groups